A HISTORY OF
CHEAM AND SUTTON

A HISTORY OF

THE OLD VILLAGES

OF

CHEAM AND SUTTON

which, with part of

THE PARISH OF CUDDINGTON

NOW FORM THE

BOROUGH OF SUTTON AND CHEAM

BY

CHARLES J. MARSHALL, F.R.I.B.A.

WITH A NEW ADDENDUM AND INDEX

BY

H. V. MOLESWORTH ROBERTS, A.L.A.

Republished by
S. R. Publishers Ltd., 1971

First published by
Cryer's Library, Cheam, Surrey, 1936

Bibliographic Note.

Addendum and Index

The addendum, bringing the story up-to-date, appears after page 105, which (apart from the index) was the last page in the original edition. A new, extended, index has been prepared for this edition, and follows the addendum.

© 1971 S.R. Publishers Limited.
East Ardsley, Wakefield,
Yorkshire, England

ISBN 0 85409 649 3

Reproduced and Printed by
Redwood Press Limited,
Trowbridge & London.

LORD JOHN LUMLEY.

From a portrait which hung in
the Lumley Chapel till 1801,
and is now at Lumley Castle.

A HISTORY OF
THE OLD VILLAGES

OF

CHEAM AND SUTTON

which, with part of

THE PARISH OF CUDDINGTON

NOW FORM THE

BOROUGH OF SUTTON AND CHEAM.

BY

CHARLES J. MARSHALL, F.R.I.B.A. (Retired).

FOR THE AUTHOR,

Published by

CRYER'S LIBRARY,

Station Road, Cheam, Surrey,

1936.

FOREWORD

—o—

A S the *History of the Village of Cheam*, which I wrote in collaboration with the late Miss Maud Roberts-West, is now out of print, I have been asked to write a revised edition and to include a history of the Village of Sutton (the two places having now been amalgamated), so as to put on record some of the traditions and descriptions of the places before it is too late and they are entirely modernised. Having lived in Sutton from 1895 to 1901, and since then in Cheam, I have seen many great changes in both places, and have spoken with many who have known the place long before I did. I have been greatly assisted by many friends, and desire to record my thanks to them all—particularly to the following: Messrs. F. Worker (for assistance with the drawings), H. Bolton, R. D. Mighell, H. Sharp, H. Bawtree, A. Rides; the Southern Railway Co., and the Water, Gas, and Electric Light Companies for much useful information, for the use of photographs, etc.

CHARLES J. MARSHALL,

" Balvaird,"

November,   20, Burdon Lane,

    1936.   Cheam, Surrey.

BOOKS CONSULTED.

A Brief History of the Parish of Cheam to 1809, by Bruce Thorns, published by the *Croydon Guardian*, North End, Croydon, 1909.

Notes on the Lumley Monuments, by George Clinch, F.S.A. Scot., F.G.S., reprinted from *Surrey Archæological Collections*, Vol. XXII, 1909.

Monumental Memoranda from Cheam Church, by Alfred Heales, F.S.A., and William W. King, reprinted from *Surrey Arch. Coll.*

A Few Notes on Banstead Downs, by Harold Bawtree, 1928.

Manning and Bray, 1808.

Lyson's *Environs of London*, 1796.

The Victoria History of Surrey.

Brayley's *History of Surrey*, 1841.

Greater London.

The Dictionary of National Biography.

The Index of Deeds in the Record Office.

Surrey Archæological Collections (Surrey Archæological Society).

Church's *Guide to Sutton*, 1869 *and* 1878.

ILLUSTRATIONS

—o—

IN THE TEXT.

INTRODUCTION.

Along the northern edge of the North Downs, where the chalk dips under the London clay, there is a narrow bed of Thanet sands extending from Croydon to Epsom. North of this belt of sand is the London clay, and south of it is chalk many hundreds of feet thick, so thick that it was impossible to get water by sinking wells. The water that could be obtained on the London clay was chiefly surface water and was not good, but on the belt of Thanet sands any amount of excellent water could be obtained from wells. This fact was discovered at a very early date, and settlements were made all along this sand belt from Croydon to Epsom, *viz.*, Waddon, Wallington, Carshalton, Sutton, Cheam, Cuddington, Ewell, Epsom, and small villages were founded at these spots.

When the Saxons came to England and began to settle it, the whole country was divided into Parishes. The usual arrangement of these Parishes was, that they were laid out as squares, with the Church, Manor-house and village in the centre, the cultivated fields round these and the common grazing grounds on the outside. Along this belt of sand, however, this arrangement would not do, as the villages were so close together; so, instead of making the Parishes square, they were made long and narrow, still having the Church, Manor-house and village in the centre, and the cultivated fields next to these, and the common grazing ground beyond; so all these parishes are about three miles long and three quarters of a mile wide. In the case of both Cheam and Sutton these commons have now disappeared, as they were enclosed under an Act of 1806 in the case of Cheam, and 1809 in the case of Sutton.

Until about the middle of the eighteenth century the North Downs extended from Epsom on the east to Croydon on the west, and from Reigate on the south to north of the Cheam Road and Carshalton Road on the north.

The North Downs must have been a very bare, desolate expanse except in some spots, such as Banstead, Burgh Heath, Walton-on-the-Hill, etc., where there were deposits of sand, gravel and clay over the chalk, in which wells could be dug, and on which trees would grow. It must have been a bleak spot until quite a late date, as it is recorded that in 1796 William Ravers of Caterham, a journeyman farrier, returning home from Banstead on Christmas Day, was lost in the snow near Smitham Bottom in Woodmansterne, and the body was not found for two days. Both Cheam and Sutton must have been very isolated villages at the edge of this great stretch of Downs, with no main roads passing near them, until 1755, when the turnpike road from London to Brighton was constructed, and at the same time a turnpike road was made from Carshalton to Ewell, passing through Cheam (now the Cheam and Carshalton Roads), running through the fields at the edge of the Downs.

CHEAM ROADS.

The old road from Sutton to Cheam can be traced from Sutton High Street, down West Street, Camden Road, Tate Road, through Love Lane to Park Lane, Cheam, down Park Lane through Cheam Park, along the avenue of Nonsuch Park and via Vicarage Lane to Ewell.

In Love Lane, Cheam, there is a " Bourne " where the water rises from the Thanet Sands in some years and forms a pond, lasting for a month or two, that was called the " Boney Hole." There was another in West Street, Sutton, called " Diver's Ditch." The Sutton Water Company now has a well and pumping station at the site of the " Boney Hole," and the " Diver's Ditch " was filled up in 1866.

In Cheam, Burdon Lane and Sandy Lane are old tracks. Before the railway came and Station Road was made they joined at their south end, farther to the east than at present, and, as one road, joined Park Lane near the gates of Cheam Park, and then continued along an old track, that can still partly be traced, till it joined the London to Epsom Road somewhere westward of the Queen Victoria. This part of the road (from Park Lane to the London–Epsom Road) was disused after the Malden Road was made about 1800.

Burdon Lane, after leaving Sandy Lane, ran south-eastwards across the Downs to Lambert's Oaks, near Woodmansterne.

Sandy Lane, south of its junction with Burdon Lane, continued across the Downs to Banstead. It was an old cattle track, very much worn down and sandy.

York Road, Cheam, follows a track that continued Gander Green Lane southwards till it joined Burdon Lane near the Warren, crossed Burdon Lane, and continued on the north side of the Warren till it reached Sandy Lane, crossed Sandy Lane and wound round till it reached Ewell.

The portion of Cheam High Street from the White House to Park Lane does not seem to have been well made, and also it was on a hill, so the stage coaches coming from Sutton turned round by the White House into Park Road (then called " Red Lion Street ") and went down Park Lane, coming into the High Road again by Cheam Park.

Manor Road follows the line of a track which branched off from Burdon Lane and joined Love Lane, following the line of Manor Road and the bye-pass road. When the railway came and crossed this track, an occupation bridge was provided for the use of the farmer of Church House Farm, who cultivated the triangular piece of land bounded by the railway, Burdon Lane and York Road. This bridge was called " Hales' Bridge," after Mr. Hales, who was then tenant of the farm. This bridge has now been replaced with the bye-pass bridge.

SUTTON ROADS.

Before the present Carshalton Road was made, the main track from Sutton to Carshalton left the Sutton High Street by the side of the Greyhound, where there is still a right of way to St. Barnabas' Road, and so on to Carshalton.

Probably also before the present Cheam and Carshalton Roads were made in 1755, there may have been a track through the open common-fields following much the same line as the present roads.

The Sutton High Street was part of a road running from Morden through Sutton on to Banstead Downs, a road from Mitcham joining it on the north side of Sutton. This track followed much the same line as the Brighton Road, and branched a short way south of Sutton Lodge as it now does, one branch following much the same line as the present Brighton Road, the other going over the Downs till it joined the continuation of Burdon Lane.

The new turnpike roads were generally made sixty feet wide, with a metalled portion in the middle for vehicles, and grass borders on each side, so that cattle could get a feed as they were driven to market. The Brighton Road appears to have been made sixty feet wide, but the Cheam and Carshalton Roads were thirty feet wide.

The Brighton Road through Sutton was the main road to that part of the South Coast until 1807, when nine miles of road was made from Croydon to Reigate, which had the great advantage of avoiding the steep pull up Reigate Hill. This, of course, greatly affected the traffic through Sutton, and diminished the tolls taken for the upkeep of the road. It was therefore provided that the Trustees of the Croydon–Reigate Road should pay £200 a year to the Trustees of the Sutton–Reigate Road as compensation.

Toll Bars.

There seem to have been four toll bars in Sutton. One was on the Brighton Road, beside the " Cock," and one on the Cheam Road, at right angles to it, the same toll house serving for both. The toll bar on the Brighton Road was moved further south, to a spot between the present Egmont Road and Sutton Lodge, either in 1840 or in 1863. The evidence for the 1840 date is that in a law suit that was held in 1878 regarding the privilege that Sutton residents had of being free from paying tolls in Sutton, it was stated that the toll bar had been removed to its new position forty years ago. The evidence in favour of 1863 is that there was no object in moving it before that date, as there were no buildings south of it (except Sutton Lodge) before then.

The toll bar on the Cheam Road was also beside the " Cock," but was moved further west to the end of Gander Green Lane in 1863, as building was then commenced westward of the Brighton Road.

The toll bar in the Carshalton Road was situated a little east of Sutton Court, where the police station now stands. When building development took place about 1845 to 1860

Toll-bar at the "Cock," Sutton, 1790.

Toll-Bar on Brighton Road in 1865.

round the Lind and St. Barnabas' Roads the toll bar was probably
moved further east towards Carshalton.

The most northerly toll bar on the Brighton Road stood on
Rose Hill.

Sutton residents were free from Sutton tolls until 1878,
when the privilege was taken away from them. The residents
brought an action against the Highways Board to recover their
privilege, but they lost their case. Toll bars were abolished
in 1882 and soon afterwards the toll houses were pulled down.
However, there is a building on the north side of the Carshalton

TOLL GATE ON CHEAM ROAD, SUTTON,
from a sketch by T. Maisey, 1834.

Road about where the toll bar stood, that looks as if it might
be part of the old toll house.

In Unwin's *Guide to Croydon and the North Downs,* published about 1840, there is the following account of the road
from Carshalton to Sutton :

> Between Carshalton and Sutton the ground continues
> to rise, and deep chalk pits on either hand show the rambler
> the depth (yet only part of the depth) of the calcarius

formation of the spur of North Downs over which he is passing. The largest and deepest of these excavations is on the left hand, and at this point the road resembles a causeway across a ravine, with only a wooden railing and some brambles being between the road and a perpendicular descent of probably forty feet on both sides.

POPULATION.

The following list shows the population of Cheam and Sutton for the last 130 years:

				CHEAM		SUTTON
1801	..	..	..	616	..	579
1811	..	..	..	757	..	638
1821	..	..	..	792	..	811
1831	..	..	..	997	..	1,121
1841	..	..	..	1,109	..	1,304
1851	..	..	..	1,137	..	1,387
1861	..	..	..	1,156	..	3,186
1871	..	..	..	1,629	..	6,558
1881	..	..	..	2,117	..	10,334
1891	..	..	..	2,146	..	13,977
1901	..	..	..	3,404	..	17,223
1911	..	..	..	6,200	..	21,270
1921	..	..	..	7,843	..	21,063
1931	..	..	..	18,510	..	27,978

In 1935 the total number of houses in the Borough was 18,863, and the population was estimated to be 76,772.

In Norman times Cheam would have about 300 inhabitants and Sutton about 200, and though in 1801 this number had doubled in the case of Cheam, and nearly trebled in the case of Sutton, they were still very small villages, with about 100 houses in each. The reason why Sutton had increased more than Cheam was owing, no doubt, to the new toll road to Brighton, made in 1755, passing through Sutton, and as horses would be changed there, employment would be given to many stablemen and others required to look after the horses. Still, in spite of this coaching industry in Sutton, Cheam was a little larger than Sutton in 1801.

Between 1801 and 1841 there was a great increase of population of both Cheam and Sutton, but Sutton had increased more than Cheam, owing, no doubt, to the increasing popularity of Brighton causing more traffic on the road, and thus giving work for more people. About 1820 it is recorded that twenty coaches passed through Sutton in a day, and in addition there would be many postchaises and private carriages.

Between 1841 and 1851 there was an increase of only twenty-eight in the inhabitants of Cheam, and eighty-three in the case of Sutton, though the Sutton railway station was opened on May 10th, 1847. The coming of the railway seems to have aroused a good deal of opposition. A sermon was preached in Cheam Parish Church, and afterwards printed, calling upon the parishioners to do all they could to prevent a railway coming into the neighbourhood, as it would upset the place and disturb the quiet of the Sundays.

Between 1851 and 1861 Cheam increased by only nineteen inhabitants, while Sutton increased by 1,799. It must be remembered that until 1863 there were no houses except the " Cock " and Sutton Court between the railway station and a line on the level of St. Nicholas' Road, for no houses could be built beyond the Thanet Sands, as water could not be obtained on the chalk. A good deal of building must, of course, have gone on to accommodate these new people, but it appears all to have been about the Lind Road district, and was called the " New Town." In Cheam the smallness of the increase can be explained by few building sites being available, the existing village being hemmed in on the east and west where were the water-bearing Thanet Sands, by Cheam Park on the west, and Cheam Manor on the east.

In Cheam at this time the only house on the chalk, south of Cheam Court Farm and Cheam School, which were on the most southerly edge of the Thanet Sands, was the old Tudor cottage at the Warren, which had a well 6 ft. by 4 ft. by 200 ft. deep.

In 1863 the Sutton Water Company was incorporated, and mains were laid up the Brighton Road and along the Cheam and Carshalton Roads, and shortly afterwards to Cheam. Wherever the mains were laid water was available and consequently all the chalk and London clay land was made available for building. Mr. Alcock, who lived at Sutton Court, being Lord of the Manor and owning a great deal of the land in Sutton south of the railway, immediately began to sell some of his land for building, and Sutton grew very rapidly.

Between 1861 and 1871 both Sutton and Cheam increased very quickly, Sutton increasing its population by 100% and Cheam by 50%.

Between 1871 and 1881 both Sutton and Cheam increased very largely, but Sutton increased more than Cheam. This can be accounted for by Sutton having a much better train service to London Bridge and Victoria than Cheam had. In 1881 the number of trains from Cheam to London (London Bridge and Victoria) was thirty-nine on weekdays and fourteen on Sundays, while from Sutton the number was sixty-seven on weekdays and twenty-one on Sundays. As most of the main line trains divided at Sutton, half going to Victoria and half to London Bridge, running without stop from Sutton to London, while all the trains from Cheam stopped at every station, Sutton had a great advantage over Cheam for residential purposes for those whose work lay in town, and this is reflected in the growth of the population. In 1909 Cheam station was rebuilt and the train service much improved, because many trains that formerly ran express to Sutton and stopped there (not going on to Cheam) were now continued on to Cheam, so that Cheam had a much better and faster service to town than it had had before. From 1911 to 1921 the population of Cheam increased by over 1,600, while that of Sutton declined by over 200. As far as Cheam is concerned this can be accounted for by the improved train service and by more building land coming into the market, and by Cheam, then under the Epsom Rural Council, having more reasonable and up-to-date building bye-laws, the old building bye-laws of the Sutton Urban Council at that time being in many respects quite out of date. The decline in the population of Sutton may partly be attributed to the South Metropolitan District Schools being given up, with their large number of children, and the buildings not having yet been taken over by the Industrial Colony.

Between 1921 and 1931 the population of Cheam more than doubled, rising from 7,843 in 1921 to 18,510 in 1931, an increase of 10,667, while that of Sutton rose from 21,063 to 27,978, an increase of 6,915. A great deal of this increase was owing to the improved train service, and, in the case of Cheam, to more land being available for building.

In 1925 the line from London Bridge to Sutton, via Croydon, was electrified, and by 1928 the lines from Victoria and London Bridge, via Mitcham, were electrified both to Sutton and Cheam.

The line from Worcester Park to Waterloo, which had been opened in 1859, was also electrified at this period.

The line from Sutton to Wimbledon was opened in 1930, giving two more stations in Cheam, viz., West Sutton in Gander Green Lane, and Sutton Common in Sutton Common Road.

During this period the omnibus service also was greatly improved, particularly that giving communication between Sutton and Cheam and the underground railway services at Morden. The following table shows the improvement in the train service from 1881 to 1936, which improvement has a direct influence on the growth of population :

Trains to London (Victoria and London Bridge)	1881	1936
Cheam—Weekdays	39	97
Sundays	14	67
Sutton—Weekdays	67	269
Sundays	21	135

CHEAM

Cheam must have been settled at an early period. Until recently there were remains of hut circles on Banstead Downs, at the top of Sandy Lane, and there were signs of a dew pond on the west side of Sandy Lane till about 1930. British and Roman pottery was found in Manor Lane in 1913 and 1924, which can be seen in the collection in the Old Cottage.

A few years ago, when the Cuddington Golf Course was being made, a human skeleton was uncovered. The author was sent for immediately, but unfortunately, though he got there within an hour of the discovery, the burial had been destroyed and the skeleton broken up. The body was that of a Saxon, and had rested on a bed of hard core composed of unworked flints and bits of flue tiles with a basket-work pattern on them, obviously taken from the ruins of a Roman house. Evidently when the burial took place these ruins must have been lying not very far away. It could not have been at that actual spot because it was on the chalk, and water could not have been obtained except by a very deep well; but it could not have been very far away, because the flints and tiles would have to be carried to the burial place. The site of the house must therefore have been on the Thanet Sands near the burial, but it has not yet been discovered, though some likely spots have been tried, two of which yielded some bits of pottery similar to that found with the burial. There are some other likely spots to try whenever opportunity offers, and it is to be hoped that whoever finds it will appreciate his discovery and excavate it properly, because, judging from the design on the flue tiles, the house must have been an important one. Roman coins have been found on Howell Hill, which is not very far from the site of the burial.

Cheam (Anglo-Saxon AE-Ham) is spelt in old documents in about fourteen different ways, among them being Cheyham, Kaham, Cheiham, or Keyham. Before 1018 Cheam belonged to the under-kings and was held by the Abbot and Convent of Chertsey, but on that date was given by Athelstan, younger son of Ethelred II and brother of Edmund Ironside, to Christ

Church, Canterbury. Bishop Lanfranc, who was Archbishop from 1070 to 1089, divided the parish into two manors, East and West Cheam. East Cheam, together with the advowson of the church, he kept to himself, and West Cheam was allotted to the monks.

In the Domesday Survey of 1086 Cheam is thus described:

The Archbishop himself holds Ceiham (Cheam) for the sustenance of the Monks. In the time of Edward (the Confessor) it was assessed for 20 hides, and now for 4 hides. The land is for 14 ploughs. In demesne there are 2 ploughs: and (there are) 25 villeins and 12 cottars with 15 ploughs. There is a church: and 5 serfs 1 acre of meadow, wood with 25 hogs. In the time of King Edward and afterwards it was worth 8 pounds, now 14 pounds.

A " plough-land " was as much land as a man could till in a year with one plough and team. " Villeins " were labourers who had a certain portion of land allotted to them, for which they were dependent on their lord, and bound to do certain work and corporeal service. " Cottars " were a class with slightly superior privileges. A " Hide " was a piece of land from 60 to 100 acres.

This would seem to show that the inhabitants of Cheam at that time would number about 300 and that there would be about fifty houses.

In 1291 Pope Nicholas gave one tenth of the ecclesiastical revenues of Cheam to King Edward I for the Crusades. From East Cheam this amounted to £10, and from West Cheam £6 13s. 4d.

Though the Archbishop claimed most of the privileges of the Lord of the Manor at Cheam, some of the officers of the Parish, such as Tithingman, Ale-taster, and Constable, were appointed from Merstham.

In 1268 Robert, son of Ralph de Fraxino de Cheyham, gave the Prior of Canterbury a piece of land. The witnesses to the deed were Simon de Cheyham, John de Cudington and Peter de Cheyham.

In the reign of Henry II (1154–1189) the Parson of Cheam was named Postell. A certain Vavassour (the rank next below that of Baron) held land at Kaham of Ralph de Kaham, but for some crime the land was forfeited and passed into the hands of Postell. An action was brought, but Postell got Ralph to say that he gave the land to the Church at Keyham. Ralph de Greville married the daughter of Postell, though his wife was still alive. She was tried for bigamy and excommunicated, and her two sons brought an action to recover the land. They were awarded their father's property but not the land belonging to their mother in Keyham.

The following list of Place Names may be of interest; some of them still exist. In a grant from William Fromond to Bartholomew Fromond dated 12 July 1560 are found:

Hasdell Close	Pylford Bridge	Sivynker
Bassetland	Fylesfeld	Pyghtell
Hackard's Close	Spensares	Bell Yard
Little Moreland	The Gate	Rythe
Mareland	Bassett Lane	Longland
Lamp Close	Dobbescroft Pit	
Little Bassett	Shepehacksfeld	

A close of land called Cockfeld and Sparfeld.

Two mills are mentioned in a fire of 1583.

In the thirty-fifth year of Henry VIII Thomas Carwarden was appointed Steward of Nonsuche, Ewell, Estchaym, West-chayam, Sutton, Banstead, and Walton-super-montem.

Preparations for the expected invasion by the Spanish Armada began in 1583, although the Armada did not actually sail till 1588. Troops were raised all over the country, and Surrey had to furnish 1,000 men. The accounts show that there was some re-arrangement of equipments among the men enlisted, and men from Cheam and Sutton are mentioned in connection with the following items:

CHEYHAM. Phillip Martin his sword was take away by the Lieutenant Mr. Pavet and his dager by the Clerk of the Band, he was served with a corslet.
Avery Maye his murrain (headpiece) was take away by the lieutenant Mr. Pavet and changed his flax and gave him a worse for it, he served with a caliver (a sort of musket).

SUTTON. Walter Gawyn his Murryan and coat take away by the lieutenant Mr. Pavet his flax and Tootchbox was take away by Sir Edward Stanles Lieutenant he served with a caliver.

Cottage in Cheam Warren. Demolished 1930 (*see* p. 22).

Church Cottage, Cheam (*see* p. 40).

Robert Bedford his sword and dager was take away by Sir Edward Stanles Lieutenant he served with a halbert.

In 1637 soldiers were levied in Surrey for service in the Low Countries, and of these one William Sidman came from Cheam. The Ship Money assessment of Cheam in 1636 was £18.

In 1625 King Charles I raised a loan for war purposes, and to this Henry Flood of Cheam gave £10 and Bartholomew Fromond £40. Sir Richard Weston of Sutton gave £20.

EAST CHEAM MANOR. East Cheam, Nether Cheam or Lower Cheam, as it is called in old deeds, lies between Cheam and Sutton at the east end of Cheam Parish, and consisted of East Cheam Manor and about a dozen houses. This was the part of Gander Green Lane from Cheam Road to Tate Road, and a little further north down Gander Green Lane.

In 1539 Cranmer exchanged East Cheam with Henry VIII for Chislet Park in Kent. In the first year of Queen Mary East Cheam was granted to Anthony Montague, who sold it to Henry, Earl of Arundel, in 1583. On the Earl's death it passed to his heir John, Lord Lumley, whose first wife had been the Earl's daughter Jane, who had died in 1576. Lord Lumley was therefor the Lord of the Manor of both East and West Cheam.

John Yerde held the lease of East Cheam Manor from Archbishop Cranmer, and when he died the Manor passed to Thomas Fromond, who was married to John Yerde's daughter and heiress. Thomas Fromond built the East Cheam Manor House which stood on the west side of Gander Green Lane, opposite the cricket field, where later Lower Cheam House stood. The original house, built by Thomas Fromond, appears to have been a very fine one, with a hall with wooden gallery at one end, containing a window with stained glass showing the arms of Yerde impaling those of Ellinbridge. There was a chapel, which in 1796 had been turned into a billiard room, adjoining the hall; at one end of it was a buttery and cellar, and in the parlour was a richly carved mantel-piece. The house appears to have been a fine example of Tudor domestic architecture. It was pulled down by Philip Antrobus about 1800 and Lower Cheam House was built on its site.

The Fromonds were Roman Catholics, and Thomas Fromond's great-grandson seems to have been more than once in trouble

for hiding Jesuits. In 1615 information was laid against
Bartholomew Fromond of Cheam for lodging a Jesuit for three
nights, one Henry Flood. In 1628 Francis Smith, aged almost
fourscore years, was released from a long imprisonment and
went at once to Fromond's house. Again in 1633 information
was laid against Bartholomew Fromond for harbouring one
Henry Flood, *alias* Francis Smith, *alias* Rogers, *alias* Seymour.

It is not known if this gentleman with the many names
was any relation of the Lloyds at West Cheam Manor House,
but certainly in 1628 Henry Lloyd, *alias* Fludd, was living there.
According to the *Victoria History*, the Lloyds had Romanist
sympathies.

The estate passed from father to son till about 1650, when
the only daughter and heiress succeeded. She had married
Richard Walmisley. The estate passed on next to Bartholomew
Walmisley, who died in 1701, leaving one son, Francis. Francis
Walmisley died in 1711, leaving one daughter, Catherine, who
in 1712, at the age of 15, married Robert, Lord Petre, who
died the following year, leaving one son, who afterwards became
Lord Petre. In 1733 Catherine was married for the second
time to Charles Stourton, who in 1743 succeeded to the title of
Lord Stourton.

Lady Petre's house was searched on Dec. 22nd, 1745, and
one Joseph Morgan Hawley was found in a concealed part of
the house. He was examined on Dec. 24th: it is not known
who he was or what he had done, but probably he was concerned
in the 1745 rebellion. Lady Petre's house was again searched
on Jan. 1st, 1746.

Cheam people seem to have been much mixed up with
political plots from time to time. In a list of suspected persons
in 1655-56 in London and Westminster, the name of William
Howard of Cheam is mentioned, and there is a letter about
him that seems to show that he had to report his movements
to the Government officials :

William Howard of Cheam Esq.
Honble Sir,

William Howard of Cheam in the Countie of Surrey
Esq on the 9th present Certified the place of his lodging

and his intention on the 10th to remove backe towards Cheam aforesaid.

London 17th July 1656

These to his Honble friend Ma
Genl, Kelsey present.

Again in London on 19th he intends to remove back 22nd.

It is not known who this William Howard was, but he evidently was known to have Royalist tendencies.

Catherine, Lady Stourton, died in 1785 at the age of 88, and upon her death her son, Lord Petre, sold the estate to Mr. Bullock, who sold it again afterwards to John Antrobus, whose son Phillip pulled down the old house about 1800 and built Lower Cheam House on its site. A portrait of Phillip Antrobus, in a velvet coat and bag wig, used to hang over the dining-room fireplace of Lower Cheam House.

The Antrobuses were made baronets during the Napoleonic wars. The second Sir Edmund Antrobus lived at Cheam for many years and was succeeded by his second son, Hugh Lindsay Antrobus, and on the latter's death in 1899 the house and estates were sold.

Mr. Ralph Beck, of the White House, Cheam, who bought the house, pulled down the third wing, the house having been built on three sides of a square.

The house was sold to Mr. Bainbridge, whose family lived in it till it was sold and pulled down in 1933, and the site is now laid out for a number of houses.

In the two large drawing-rooms, which opened out of each other, there was a wonderful Chinese wall-paper. It was brought from China by a ship's captain, who sold it to Sir Edmund Antrobus, who had it put up about 1826. It represented some Chinese story, which began at one corner and worked round two rooms. No two details were alike. The figures were all different; there were wonderful and curious-looking animals, while higher up on the walls in the tree branches were fantastic birds. The paper was of great value and was removed from the walls before the house was pulled down, but it is not known where it is now.

There were at least two other such wall-papers. One was at Minto in Scotland, but it has now been taken down. The other is at Sir Walter Scott's home, Abbotsford, and is an exact replica of the one that was at Lower Cheam House.

Since 1765 the Northey family have been the Lords of the Manor. Memorials to most of the owners of East Cheam Manor are to be found in the Lumley Chapel.

WEST CHEAM MANOR. The tenants of West Cheam Manor, of whom there were seven, held their lands on condition of doing certain services. Each was to plough half an acre or give 5d. Each having a horse was to harrow oats one day. All were to perform 602 days' work or give 25s. 1d. The price of two works was fixed at 1d. Works were not to be done for two weeks at Christmas, one at Easter and one at Pentecost. Each was to work for two days a week for five weeks at harvest. The cottars were to do 688 works or to give 19s. 2d.; three works were valued at 1d. Mowing one acre of wheat or oats equalled two works, mowing one acre of barley, pease, or tares, equalled four works. In harvest each cottar had to perform 150 works. The tenants, when they did their services, were allowed one bushel of rye or barley, herrings to the value of 12d. and cheese 3d. The harrowers had one bushel of barley and herrings to the value of 6d.

West Cheam Manor, which was held for the monks of Canterbury, came to Henry VIII on the dissolution of the monasteries. In 1585 Queen Elizabeth granted the Manor of West Cheam to John, Lord Lumley, with the exception of the lead and bells of the Church, and the advowson of the Church, which latter went with East Cheam Manor.

Lord John Lumley was the son of George Lumley, who was beheaded for being concerned in an insurrection against Henry VIII. Lord John Lumley was married first to Jane, daughter and heiress of the Earl of Arundel, and secondly to Elizabeth, daughter of Lord D'Arcy of Chiche. Lord Lumley died in 1609 without leaving any surviving children, and the estate passed to Henry Lloyd, son of Lord Lumley's sister Barbara. On Henry Lloyd's death the estate passed to his son, also named Henry, who died in 1704, leaving the estate to his son Robert. Robert took Holy Orders and by the favour of the Duke of Bedford he was given the living of St. Paul's, Covent Garden. He published a poem to King William in 1689, and two sermons in 1709 and 1711. In

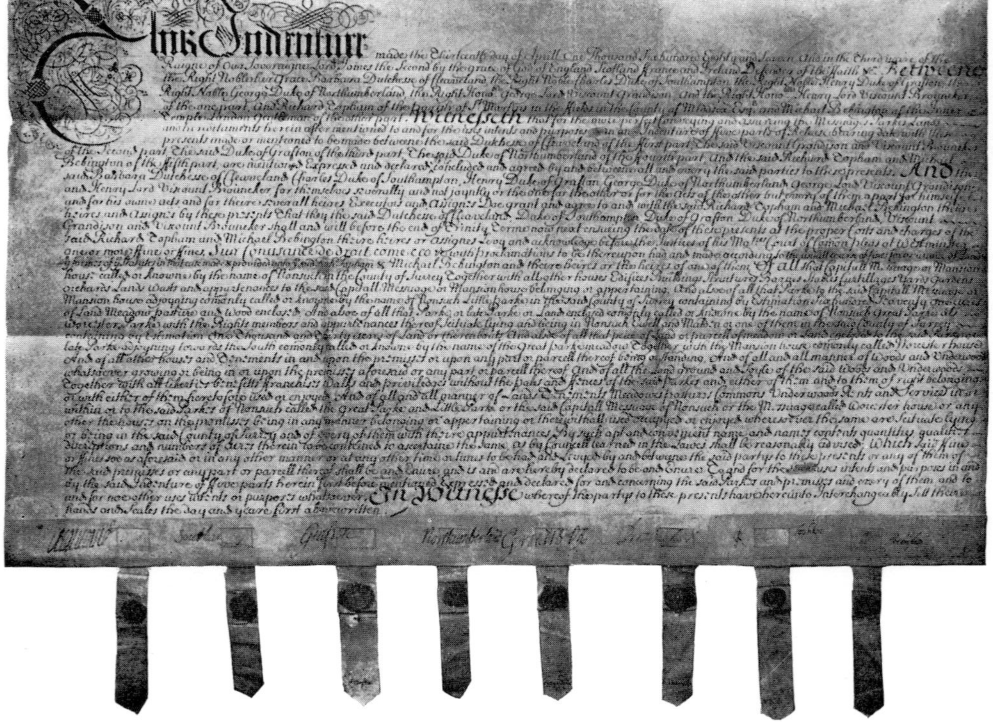

Deed of Sale of Nonsuch

1723 he laid claim to the Barony of Lumley, as being descended from one of the daughters of George, Lord Lumley, but was opposed by the Earl of Scarborough and lost his case. His death occurred a little after 1730, and by his will he left the estate to his patron, the Duke of Bedford. The Duke of Bedford sold the estate to Edward Northey, of Woodcote House, Epsom, for £22,340. Edward Northey had been Solicitor General in 1710. The Northey family have been the lords of the manor ever since.

West Cheam Manor House stood in the square of ground bounded by Malden Road, Park Road, Church Street and Church Road. There are no remains of the house and no description of it, except that it was standing in 1796, that it was built of brick, and that it was in a bad state of repair. It was pulled down soon after 1796. There are some stables, now used for stores by the Sutton and Cheam Borough Council, which are situated on the south side of the footpath by the side of the churchyard, opposite Church Farm House, which were part of the stables of West Cheam Manor. They are built of squared chalk blocks. Part of the wall on the west side of Church Street, dividing the street from the Borough Council's stores, is also built of squared chalk blocks. Formerly a brick wall, some twelve feet high, went round the grounds of the Manor House. In Park Road it stood where the railings of the front gardens of the houses now are. At the corner of Park Road and the Malden Road, where the Baptist Chapel now stands, there were several blocked-up windows in this wall, showing that there were some of the outbuildings of the Manor there. The wall was continued about twelve feet high along Malden Road and up Church Road, and was pulled down to its present level when the War Memorial was built in part of the garden of the Manor. The exact site of the house is not known.

A very fine octagonal brick pigeon house, with ogee lead roof, stood in the grounds of the Manor until about 1902, but it was pulled down when the houses in Park Road were built. It stood nearly behind " Inlandes."

There is a legend in the parish that a family of Huguenots, who had fled from France at the time of the massacre of St. Bartholomew, established a silk factory in East Cheam Manor and there wove the first silk stockings made in England and presented them to Elizabeth when she was at Nonsuch. The garden surrounded by its wall was always called the " Factory Garden."

No documentary evidence of this fact has yet been discovered, and it is difficult to understand how the story arose and how it was connected particularly with West Cheam Manor. The house was continually inhabited and it is not easy to understand how a silk-weaving factory could have been established there. One explanation would be that a silk-weaving factory was established somewhere in Cheam, and it is possible that the Duke of Bedford's factor lived in West Cheam Manor House and that the house might thus be called "the factor's house"; this might become "the factory house" and the existing story of the silk-weaving factory be transferred to it. Among the names of the families long resident in Cheam there do not seem to be any of a French origin.

It is stated that after the Duke of Bedford's period of residence there was a paper factory erected. Paper-making in those days without water power was conducted at a loss and the factory closed down after a few years.

Cheam acquired great importance from its proximity to the Palace of Nonsuch, and though this was in the parish of Cuddington, yet the history of Cheam was so much bound up with that of the Palace, and of its owners, that it would be well to give here a short account of Nonsuch Palace.

NONSUCH. Henry VIII purchased a large estate, including the village and church, in the neighbouring parish of Cuddington, from Sir Richard Codington in 1537. In 1538 he commenced building a large palace or hunting box, and to clear the site he pulled down the village and church of Cuddington. The building was only half finished when Henry VIII died in 1547. It was designed by a Florentine architect and was a magnificent structure, hence its fancy name of "Nonsuch." The buildings, which were of brick, timber and stucco, were grouped round a courtyard, 137 feet broad and 116 feet long, and were the wonder of their time. When Elizabeth came to the throne she sold "Nonsuch" to the Earl of Arundel, who greatly enlarged it, the additions he built being larger than the original structure. These new buildings were grouped round a second courtyard, 150 feet long and 132 feet wide. After the death of the Earl of Arundel "Nonsuch" passed to John, Lord Lumley, his son-in-law. The estate was much impoverished by all this building,

Photo by G. Thorns.

Entrance to Nonsuch.   Showing Tudor Garden Wall.

Photo by W. Hooper.

Pigeon House, formerly in grounds of West Cheam Manor.
(Demolished 1902) (*see* p. 17).

and Lord Lumley had borrowed from Queen Elizabeth. Elizabeth pressed him for payment, and as Lord Lumley was rather under a cloud, as he had been mixed up in a conspiracy connected with a plot to marry Mary Queen of Scots to the Duke of Norfolk, for which he was imprisoned, Lord Lumley agreed to sell " Nonsuch " to Elizabeth in consideration of the cancelling of the debt. Lord Lumley was appointed Custodian of " Nonsuch," so he continued to reside there, though at the same time he held the manors of both East and West Cheam. Both Henry VIII and Elizabeth paid many visits to " Nonsuch." At the time of the Fire of London in 1666 the Exchequer was moved down to " Nonsuch," and Pepys visited the house and park and describes it in his diary. It was also visited by James I and by Charles I.

The Palace of Nonsuch was given by Charles II to Lady Castlemaine in 1669, whom he created Duchess of Cleveland and Baroness Nonsuch. She, being heavily in debt, pulled the palace down, turned the park into farm lands, and sold the contents and materials for building purposes. The deed of sale is now hanging in the Old Cottage.

There are very few remains of the Palace. It stood where the present road through Nonsuch Park turns at right angles towards the London Road. This present road runs right through the centre of the two court-yards, and a depression in the road marks the gateway between the two courts. In " Cherry Orchard Farm," to the south of the site of the Palace, are the remains of the wall of the private gardens. The footpath to Ewell runs on the top of this wall. On the south side of this footpath is a deep depression, which is the site of the stables or of some sunk garden. In the grounds of Ewell Castle are the remains of the Summer Banqueting Hall. It is shaped rather like a fort, with circular bastions and with a low parapet wall round it. In the centre is a mound, which marks the site of a three-storey pavilion which was built of wood. There are broad terraces round this pavilion, and they were probably used for theatricals and masques. It is possible that Shakespeare himself may have taken part in some of the masques when Elizabeth was holding her court at " Nonsuch."

It was at " Nonsuch " that Sir Walter Raleigh courted Elizabeth Throgmorton, daughter of Sir Nicholas Throgmorton and niece of Francis Carew of Beddington, who was a Lady-in-Waiting or Maid-of-Honour to Queen Elizabeth. Raleigh married her in 1592, and Queen Elizabeth immediately committed him to the Tower.

Probably a part of the old Palace was left standing for a time. Joseph Thompson lived at "Nonsuch" in 1730 till his death in 1743. His nephew, Joseph Whately, Vicar of Widford, Herts., the father of Richard Whately, Archbishop of Dublin, was there in 1780. He altered the gardens considerably and wrote a book entitled *Observations on Modern Gardening.* He died in 1797.

The land was then bought by Mr. Samuel Farmer, in whose family it has remained ever since. He built the present castellated house in 1802–5 from designs by Sir Geoffrey Wyattville. It was added to in 1845.

The first lilac trees were brought to "Nonsuch" by Sir Walter Raleigh. The late Hon. Mrs. Francis Colborne kept up the old tradition, as every known kind of lilac is at present growing in the gardens of Nonsuch Park.

The house was built considerably nearer to Cheam than the old Palace. By the front door there is a stone let into the wall, with an inscription and date. It is supposed to have been built over the front entrance of the old Palace.

There are some carvings at Epsom and a fireplace at Eltham, beyond which there are few remains of the old Palace. Some houses in the neighbourhood are said to be built of Nonsuch stones—among others, "The Durdans" at Epsom, "Bay Cottage" and "The Cabin" in Cheam—and traditionally the porch at "The Cedars," Peach's Close, Cheam, was built out of an old summer-house that belonged to the Palace. In Epsom Church is an old mahogany chest brought from "Nonsuch." It belonged to one of the Spanish ships in the Armada and was given by Sir Walter Raleigh to Queen Elizabeth. The dog lion on the gates of Epsom churchyard also came from "Nonsuch," and its pair is at Thurlow Towers, Dulwich.

The portion of the garden wall of the present house on the west side of the fir tree avenue leading up to the house is believed to be part of the original garden wall of the Palace.

Dr. Richard Pococke mentions in his *Travells Throughout England in 1750*, that " Charles II gave Nonsuch to the Duchess of Cleveland, who sold the materials with which the Earl of Barkeley built Durdans . . . . so that at Nonsuch there is only a farm house."

There are some curious old pictures in the library of the modern house, which were believed to have been found in the cellars. In one of them, a portrait of Queen Mary I, the queen is wearing a jewel which, when the present ex-Queen of Spain was visiting " Nonsuch " some years ago, she recognised as one of the Crown Jewels of Spain.

" Nonsuch " still keeps up its reputation for Royal visitors. Princess Beatrice was a frequent guest, and H.M. Queen Mary and Princess Mary paid a visit to " Nonsuch " in 1918.

Years ago in the park there was a beautiful old elm tree which was called Queen Elizabeth's Elm, owing to the legend that the Queen used to stand under its shadow when she was shooting deer with a cross-bow. The tree was 22 ft. 6 in. in girth and 80 ft. in height. Only a stump remained for a long time, and it was quite hollow. Unfortunately, it was entirely destroyed by fire owing to the carelessness of some boys from Ewell.

In the same field there is a rather broad ditch which goes by the name of Diana's Dyke. This is supposed to be part of the old moat of the Palace and was so named from a statue of the goddess which, tradition says, stood close by. Here a " bourne," *i.e.*, a stream which only flows once in every few years, traditionally every seven years, rises occasionally.

In 1656 the Commonwealth Government made a complete survey and valuation of Nonsuch Palace and the great and little parks. The great park was Worcester Park, and adjoined the little park, which was the one in which the Palace stood. This is part of the inventory of the little park:

> And all that Parke or Impaled Ground commonly called and knowne by the name of Nonsuch little park lying and being betweene the parishes of Ewell and Cheame in the County of Surry bounded with the town of Ewell upon the west the Common fields upon the south the town of Cheame upon the East and the greate parke upon the North, conteyning in the whole uppon admeasurement six hundred three-score and eleven acres of land worth the whole per annum £402–12–0

THE WARREN. Between Burdon Lane and Sandy Lane, at the Belmont end of the parish, is a plantation of trees surrounded by a high brick wall, built chiefly of seventeenth-century bricks, but with some parts in Tudor bricks. At the entrance stood a cottage, with the walls of the ground floor constructed of squared chalk blocks and flints, and the upper floor of timber. The ground floor was the original cottage, a very good specimen of Tudor work, and the upper floor was of seventeenth-century work. In front of the cottage was a well 6 ft. × 4 ft. and 200 feet deep. Why should such a small cottage have such a very expensive well ? The suggestion is that the well was dug in connection with the water supply to Nonsuch, as the lie of the land is such that water could gravitate down to the Palace, and that the cottage was a donkey house, as the water was probably raised by means of a wheel worked by a donkey walking round inside it, as can still be seen at Carisbrook Castle. The space enclosed by the wall, which is about eleven acres, was used as a hare warren. At intervals all round the walls are holes fitted with little sliding trap-doors. These were used for coursing hares. The idea was that the riders and dogs waited outside, while beaters drove the hares out of the warren, and coursing took place over the downs, which then extended from Epsom to Croydon and from Reigate nearly down to Cheam Road.

A few years ago efforts were made to save the cottage and the walls, which were then in danger of destruction, and the Society for the Preservation of Ancient Buildings used their influence in endeavouring to save these structures. The walls were saved and are still standing, but, though the immediate destruction of the cottage was averted, it was pulled down in 1930, and unfortunately no measured drawings of it were made.

CHEAM CHURCH. The present church, erected in 1864 from the designs of Mr. T. H. Pownall, is a brick building in the French Gothic style. The chancel screen, erected in 1931, was designed by Mr. Ryan Tenison, and formerly stood in the chapel of St. John's College, Battersea, and was presented to the Rector of St. Dunstan's, the Rev. Canon Wesley Dennis, when the chapel was pulled down, as he had been Principal of the College before coming to St. Dunstan's. At the same time that the screen was erected the walls of the chancel were panelled and new altar

Cheam Church prior to 1864. (From an old photograph.)

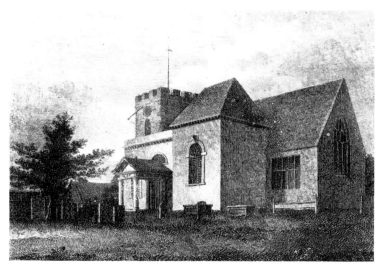

Cheam Church, 1746–1864.
(From an engraving now in the Vestry.)

23

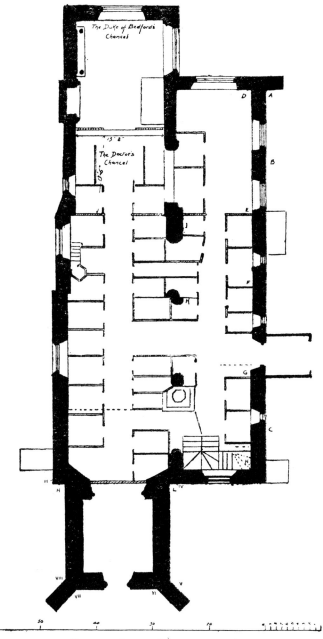

The Duke of Bedford's
Chancel

The Doctor's
Chancel

PLAN OF CHEAM CHURCH IN 1746.

rails erected, from the designs of the author and Mr. Swan of Oxted. The pulpit, which was put up at the same time as part of the screen, was presented by the late Hon. Mrs. Francis Colborne in memory of her husband.

The old church stood on the south side of the present one. The Lumley Chapel, which still stands, was the chancel, and the church extended westwards to near the tree standing by the lych gate. The position is a very prominent one, as it is on a low hill that can be seen from a long distance round, and we cannot doubt that it was the site of some place of worship from

CHEAM CHURCH IN 1862.

a very early date. In the course of some repairs to the Lumley Chapel in 1918 it was necessary to remove part of the roughcast, and the remains of two windows were discovered. These are evidently very early Norman or perhaps pre-Norman. Manning and Bray state that Lord Lumley, in 1592, erected a chapel on the north side of the chancel of Cheam Church to contain the tombs of his two wives and his own. The discovery of these two windows shows that at the time of Lord Lumley this chancel was a ruin and that what he had done was to restore this chancel.

The Lumley Chapel has a very fine plaster ceiling, with pendentives and a frieze and beam with fruit and flowers in low relief. On one of the pendentives is the date 1592. Plans in the Lumley Chapel show the two churches that have occupied this site. The first church appears to have been commenced in early Norman or pre-Norman times. The building of the chancel and the church has been extended westwards from time to time, and each time it was lengthened the addition was made a little wider than what then existed. At the west end was a square tower, which from some mouldings of the arch, as drawn on one of the plans, seems to be of fifteenth-century work. On the south side of

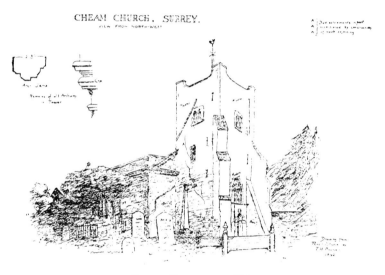

CHEAM CHURCH, SURREY.
VIEW FROM NORTH-WEST.

CHEAM CHURCH IN 1862.

the Lumley Chapel is one bay of the arcade dividing the aisle from the nave, and this is of late thirteenth-century work. The chapel at the east end of this aisle was known as the Fromond Chapel. The Fromonds lived at East Cheam Manor. The window at the east end of the Lumley Chapel was probably placed there by Lord Lumley, but its style is certainly earlier than 1592, and when the roughcast was stripped off during the repairs made in 1918 it was found that the window did not fit the arch properly, that the stones did not tail into the wall, and the sill had been cut into short pieces. From this it would appear that the window had been removed from some other position (perhaps it was the east window of the chancel that existed before Lord Lumley built his chapel), and that he moved it into his new wall further eastward. In 1639 the church was struck by lightning, but there is no record of what damage was done.

In 1746 the church got ruinous and was pulled down, except the Lumley and Fromond Chapels and the tower. The centre part of the church was rebuilt as a brick church in the classic style. The ceiling was formed in plaster and panelled. A portion

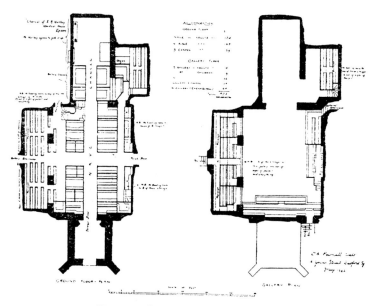

PLAN OF CHEAM CHURCH IN 1862.

of it still exists in the Lumley Chapel, showing the date 1746. This new church had five galleries, two of the galleries being approached by inside staircases, and three of them by outside stairs. In 1750 Lady Stourton rebuilt the Fromond Chapel, but did not disturb the floor, so that the gravestones remained in their original positions. The north aisle, with its galleries, was built in 1837. In 1862 it was decided to build a new church, and on its completion in 1864 the whole of the old church, with the exception of the Lumley Chapel, was pulled down. In

LUMLEY CHAPEL.

West window (*see* p. 25).   Saxon windows (*see* p. 24).

Thirteenth-century arch,   Chalk block wall
Lumley Chapel (*see* p. 25).   of West Cheam Manor (*see* p. 17).

1865, under the site of the old tower, a stone coffin was discovered with the skeleton of an old man inside, evidently a priest, as a pewter chalice and paten were lying beside him. The vestments had all disappeared, only remains of a leather girdle covered with silk and gilt, and a much corroded buckle being found. The interment was of the thirteenth century. The chalice and paten were for a considerable period in the Rectory at Cheam, but all trace of them has now disappeared. It is also not known what became of the stone coffin.

THE LUMLEY CHAPEL. On the south side of the Lumley Chapel is the monument which John, Lord Lumley, put up in 1592 to his first wife, Jane, daughter of Henry Fitzalan, eighteenth Earl of Arundel, of Nonsuch Palace. It consists of an altar-shaped tomb of alabaster with top formed of a black marble slab. On two panels on the front are carvings showing her three children, all of whom died in infancy. These figures are represented as kneeling in the interior of a building, and through an open door can be seen a monument which is like one that stood in the garden of Nonsuch, so that these must be interiors in the Palace. The clouds above probably represent their prayers going up like incense. At each end of the tomb is a shield with the Lumley and Fitzalan arms, with supporters of popin-jays (parrots) and a white horse with an oak branch in its mouth. The slab at the east end has at some time been broken and badly repaired. On the wall above this tomb is a square of alabaster with a bas-relief of Lady Lumley kneeling upon an ornamental cushion. The coif, ruff, and drapery, are carved with great care and finish, and a pomander hangs almost to her knees and is visible through an opening in her gown. This lady, who died in 1577, was learned and accomplished, and translated the *Iphigenia* of Euripides and some of the orations of Isocrates into English, and one of the latter into Latin. The MSS. are in the British Museum.

Opposite to this, on the north side of the chapel, is the beautiful monument, with a recumbent figure in alabaster, to Elizabeth, daughter of Thomas D'Arcy, Second Baron of Chiche, the second wife of John, Lord Lumley. The name of the sculptor is unknown, but from the general character of this monument, the beauty of the sculpture recalling the one to Mary Queen of Scots in Westminster Abbey, and from the date, it is possibly by the same artist.

On the north wall of the chapel is the large monument, with two marble columns, which John, Lord Lumley, put up to himself. On each side of the monument are carved shields, showing the pedigree of the Lumley family, and it bears the family motto, *Murus Æneus Sana Conscientia* ("A sound conscience is a wall of brass ").

John, Lord Lumley, was descended from a Yorkshire family that had taken a prominent part in the political movements of the time. His father, George Lumley of Thwing, in the East Riding, was executed at Tyburn for participation in Aske's insurrection. Lumley, however, inherited the family estates on the death of his grandfather, John, Lord Lumley. He was educated in the Court of Edward VI and attended the funeral of that king. He was created a Knight of the Bath; attended Queen Mary's coronation; was one of the peers who in 1553-4 sat in judgment on the Duke of Suffolk, charged with high treason; was present at the condemnation of Dr. Rowland Taylor for heresy at St. Mary Overie; sat in judgment on Charles, Lord Stourton, for the murder of Hartgylls; was one of the peers who sat upon the trial of Lord Wentworth, charged with the treasonable surrender of Calais in 1588; and was imprisoned in the Tower of London for alleged complicity in plots to set Mary Queen of Scots upon the throne. Lord Lumley was interested in a variety of pursuits. He was an antiquary, and became one of the members of the original Society of Antiquaries, founded in the reign of Elizabeth. He was High Steward of the University of Oxford, and collected a fine library, in which he was assisted by his brother-in-law Humphrey Lloyd. After his death in 1609 the books were purchased by King James I and became the foundation of the Royal Library, which now forms part of the collection in the British Museum. Lumley also took an interest in medical science. In 1582-3 he, in conjunction with Richard Caldwell, M.D., founded a surgery lecture in the Royal College of Physicians, endowing it with the yearly stipend of £40.

By a deed dated 30th April, 1597, made between Lord Lumley of the one part and William Fromond and other inhabitants of Cheam of the other part, Lord Lumley places the three monuments he had erected, *viz.*, to Lady Jane, his first wife, Lady Elizabeth, his second, and to himself, in the care of the parish of Cheam, and says:

> He hopes they may be preserved, and that there is not any person of godly disposition who will deface, destroy, or take away the same: and in consideration that the clerk be careful to sweep and rub the same monuments, and that the parson shall call upon the clerk to perform this duty, and for the relief of the poor, he grants to Fromond and others a yearly rent charge of 40 shillings issuing out of his estate here, to be paid at Lady day only of each year, of which 6*s.* 8*d.* was to be paid to the parson, 13*s.* 4*d.* to the clerk and 2*s.* each to 10 poor people.

The Earl of Scarborough is the present head of the family of Lumley.

When the old church was pulled down in 1864, all the brasses and wall monuments were removed and placed in the Lumley Chapel. On an iron stand is displayed a brass which is a palimpsest, *i.e.*, a brass that was inscribed and used, and then at a later date taken up and reinscribed on the back and used again for another person. This brass is made up of portions of several old memorials joined together and engraved on the back, to form a memorial to Thomas Fromond, Esquire, who died in 1542, in the thirty-third year of the reign of Henry VIII, and to his wife Elizabeth, daughter and heiress of John Yerde, Esquire, and their six sons and four daughters. Above is a representation of the Trinity, and also two shields, one with the arms of Fromond, and the other those of Yerde. On the back can be seen the engravings that were on the original monuments, which are portions of a figure of a lady kneeling, a shroud figure, portions of a figure under a canopy, in which is St. John the Evangelist holding a chalice from which the evil spirit is flying, and above is a representation of a heart between two hands issuing from clouds with rays proceeding from them. All these original brasses are of about 1490, though a shield with a coat of arms that is amongst them is of an earlier date. This brass was originally on the wall in the Fromond Chapel.

On the floor there are several brasses, but unfortunately they are not in their original stones. Towards the east end, on the north side of the chapel, is a brass to a civilian (*circa* 1360), but unfortunately the inscription is missing, and also a piece about 8½ in. long from the middle of the figure. It represents an elderly man with short hair and forked beard. It originally lay on the floor of the south aisle of the church, near the west end. It is possible it may be the memorial of William de Cheyham, who was a citizen of London in 1340 and 1345, though it is not recorded to which company he belonged.

On a stone, parallel with that just described, on the south side of the chapel, there are several brasses grouped together. Among these are:

A demi-figure of a civilian (*circa* 1360) which was discovered below the woodwork when the church was pulled down, and no record of it existed.

Two small demi-figures of a civilian and his wife, which were originally at the west end of the north aisle, are believed to be John Compton, died 1450, and his wife Johanna, died 1458, who are commemorated in the westernmost of the inscription tablets on this stone.

Near this is the demi-figure of a civilian which appears to be of William Wodeward, a brother of the rector of this church, died 1459. This was originally near the south door of the church.

The very small brass of a man in armour, standing sideways, is probably the smallest known brass of an adult. The date is about 1480.

There are also tablets to Barthus Fromond (1579) and to Michael Denys (1518). Also shields with the arms of Courtney and Yerde.

On the east wall is a large rectangular plate with a quaintly worded inscription to Edmund Barrett, Esquire, " Sergeant of the Wine Cellar " to King Charles I, who died in 1631, and to his first wife Dorothy Hapsley, who had three sons and two daughters, and his second wife, Ruth Causten, who had three sons and two daughters. Also to his eldest son, Thomas, who was Clerk of the Wardrobe to King Charles I and died in 1632. The inscription commences: " Reader, this marble will consume like the bodies it covers; but while it endures, know that it preserves the memory of a saint departed," and finishes: " Thus father and son are composed together in the grave of corruption: loving they were in their lives and in death they are not divided. Reader, Praise God for the happy departure of his faithful servants, and fare thee well."

MONUMENTS IN LUMLEY CHAPEL.

To the first Lady Lumley.   To Lord John Lumley.
To the second Lady Lumley.   Interior of Chapel.

On the floor is a stone in memory of Rev. J. Payne, who died in 1806. The lead plate from his coffin, with embossed ornament and his name and date, is now in the chapel. Another lead coffin plate that is in the chapel is a cast one, and was on the coffin of Sarah Best, dated 1772, who formerly resided at Cheam Cottage.

Also on the floor is a stone with inscription to Thomas Usborn, or Osborn, rector of this church, who died in 1686.

On the east wall is a marble monument to John Pybus, who died in 1789, and who was the first Englishman received by the King of Ceylon in a public character. Also on the east wall is a monument to Martha Pybus, widow of John Pybus, of Cheam, died 1802, and to Charles Small Pybus, of Cheam, one of the commissioners of Lord High Admiral, who died in 1810. John Pybus lived at Cheam House on his retirement, and it is possible that he built the house. One of his daughters married Rev. Sydney Smith, Canon of St. Paul's, and her daughter became Lady Holland.

Also on the west wall are monuments to Sir Thomas Yates of Peel Hall, Lancashire, a Judge of the King's Bench and Common Pleas, died 1770, and one to Leonard Hammond, died 1787.

On the south wall is a marble monument " sacred to the beloved innocence—Frances, the daughter of Samuel and Anna Peirson, born Sept. 30th, 1690, died May 31st, 1693." The memorial to her father, Samuel Peirson, who died in 1699, and to her mother, Anna Peirson, who died in 1728, aged 82, are on the same wall further west. This Samuel Peirson left land for the benefit of the poor of Cheam, which is described under Cheam Charities. He lived at the White House.

Near these are monuments to members of the Antrobus family, who built and lived in the present Lower Cheam House, formerly East Cheam Manor—Philip Antrobus, who died in 1816, and Sir Edmund Antrobus, of Amesbury, who died in 1826.

There is also a monument to James Bovey, who was probably connected with Cheam School, and who died in 1695.

The Sanxay family, who carried on the school from 1690, are commemorated by several monuments in the churchyard, and by two memorials in this chapel, one to Maria Sanxay, who died in 1777, who was a Miss Antrobus, and one to Maria

Davenport, daughter of Edmund and Maria Sanxay, who died suddenly in 1796.

On the east wall is a monument to Charles Mayo, who carried on Cheam School, and near it is a memorial to Henry Thomas, Fourth Earl of Carrick, who died in 1846, aged 12 years, and was interred in the same grave as his beloved tutor, Charles Mayo.

On the floor is a stone to Margaret Aldrich, third wife of George Aldrich, who was the first known master of Cheam School.

Until recently there was a very fine helmet in this chapel, the history of which was unknown, but possibly it was used at Lord Lumley's funeral; it used to stand on his tomb, but some ten or twelve years ago it mysteriously disappeared and it has never been traced.

In the churchyard there is a flat tombstone that was formerly on the floor of the old church, to the memory of Mrs. Jane Pattinson, who died in 1755, aged 66 years.

> She was Waiting Woman to her late Grace Diana, first wife of the Most Noble John, Duke of Bedford, who in regard to Mrs. Pattinson's faithful services, upon her death bed, in the year 1735, recommended her to His Grace's favour, from whom she received quarterly to the day of her death a bounty of five hundred pounds a year.

She was very charitable in the parish and some of the church plate is inscribed as having been presented by her.

The following is a list of the Rectors of Cheam since 1459:

WODEWARD. There is a brass in the Lumley Chapel in memory of his brother, who died in 1459.

JOHN WYRLEY, buried 7th September, 1581.

ANTHONY WATSON, 1581, died 1605. Bishop of Chichester 1596–1605.

THOMAS PLAYFERE, 1605, died 1609.

LANCELOT ANDREWES, 1609, resigned the same year on becoming Bishop of Ely. In 1618 he became Bishop of Winchester.

GEORGE MOUNTAIN, 1609, resigned 1617. He became Bishop of Lichfield in 1611; Bishop of Lincoln in 1619, and Archbishop of York in 1628.

RICHARD SENHOUSE, 1617, resigned 1624 on being made Bishop of Carlisle.

Figure of second Lady Lumley (*see* p. 27).

JOHN HACKET, 1624, resigned 1662 on being made Bishop of Lichfield.

JOHN DOUGHTY, 1662, died 1672.

EDWARD BERNARD, 1672, resigned 1673.

GEORGE USBORN, *alias* OSBORN, buried 8th December, 1686. There is a floor stone on his grave in the Lumley Chapel.

HENRY DAIRES, LL.D., 1686.

GEORGE PICKERNE, B.D., 1703.

WILLIAM BRIDGE, resigned (date unknown).

ABEL EVANS, D.D. Buried October 22nd, 1737.

THOMAS KEMP, D.D., 1738, an absentee. Thomas Pickerne was Curate-in-Charge.

JAMES KING, D.D., 1747, died 1780.

HENRY PEACH, B.D., 1780. There is a wall memorial to him in the Lumley Chapel. Peach's Close is named after him.

WILLIAM BENNETT, 1813.

THOMAS CARTERET MAULE, 1856.

CHARLES HOBBS RICE, 1867, died 1904.

HENRY ARTHUR WANSBROUGH, 1904, resigned 1917.

HERBERT WESLEY DENNIS, 1917, Canon of Southwark Cathedral.

In olden times Cheam seems to have excelled in the matter of rectors, for out of six successive rectors five became bishops.

Anthony Watson, rector from 1581 to 1605, was Bishop of Chichester. He is buried in Cheam, but there seems to be no grave or inscription remaining. He was Almoner to James I.

The next rector did not reach to the bishop's mitre. He was Thomas Playfere, of whom Fuller says: " His fluency in the Latin tongue seemed to be a wonder till Collins so far exceeded him." He was Margaret Professor of Divinity at Cambridge.

Next followed the famous Lancelot Andrews. He was only a year in Cheam, 1609, and resigned on becoming Bishop of Ely. Several times, when the Court was at Nonsuch, he served as Chaplain to James I. Bishop Andrews is said to have understood fifteen languages and was a celebrated preacher.

Fuller says of him: " Those who stole his sermons could

not steal his manner." A poem upon him, written at the time, was:

> If any merited to be
> The universal Bishop, this was he,
> Great Andrews, who the whole vast sea did drain
> Of learning, and distilled it in his brain.
> Those pious drops are of the purest kind
> Which trickled from the limbeck of his mind.

He is buried in St. Saviour's, Southwark.

George Mountain came to Cheam in 1609, and though he was made Bishop of Lichfield in 1611, he remained rector of Cheam till he became Bishop of Lincoln in 1619. He was Archbishop of York in 1628.

Richard Senhouse followed him in 1617 and resigned in 1624 on being made Bishop of Carlisle. He preached at the Coronation of Charles I and wrote several books, among others *Lectures on Some of the Psalms*.

Dr. John Hacket, who came next in 1624, was the last rector of Cheam to be made a bishop. He was a great collector of archives. He was rector of St. Andrew's, Holborn, and was then transferred to Cheam. Lord Keeper Williams, who presented him to this living, wrote:

> Holborn for wealth
> And Cheam for health.

Dr. Hacket was an exceedingly witty man. At the outbreak of the Civil War he was chosen by the clergy as Advocate against the Bill for taking away the Church government. He remained at Cheam till the Earl of Essex and his army, passing through Cheam, took him prisoner. The legend is that he was discovered hiding in the underground vaults at Whitehall. He refused to change his principles, and on being released he returned to Cheam, where he still continued to read the Book of Common Prayer at the church services, until forbidden by the Surrey Committee to do so. Then he only omitted those parts which might give offence to Cromwell's government.

On one occasion a soldier, entering his church, presented a pistol at his breast and ordered him to stop.

Hacket replied he would do what became a divine, let the other do what became a soldier, and continued the service.

Dr. Hacket married a niece of Sir Nicholas Carew, of Beddington.

His motto, " Serve God and be cheerful," still remains in Cheam, being written over the door of the Parochial Rooms, and it has now become the motto of the Borough of Sutton and Cheam.   He remained rector of Cheam till 1662, when he was made Bishop of Lichfield.   While at Cheam he wrote a biography of his friend and patron, Lord Keeper Williams, in which he says, somewhat ungrammatically: " Myself have been Rector of Cheam now above thirty years."   He also wrote a Latin comedy, (*Loyala*), which was twice acted before James I, but that was before coming to Cheam.

His successor, John Doughty, rector from 1662 till 1672, published some sermons and political tracts.

Edward Bernard was an astronomer and resigned the living of Cheam in 1673, when he was made Savilian Professor of Astronomy at Oxford.

Dr. James King, rector from 1747 to 1780, was a writer and a well-known wit.   He wrote a number of anecdotes.

During the eighteenth and early nineteenth centuries there were several absentee rectors.   Thomas Kemp, 1738–1747, appears to have been very little in Cheam, and his place was taken by Thomas Pickerne, curate-in-charge, and during this time the " parsonage " was let to John Bartholomew, a farmer. Mr. Barton Bouchier was another curate-in-charge, and also Mr. Wilding of Cheam School.

The patronage of the church went with East Cheam Manor, and when Cranmer exchanged that Manor for Chislet Park in 1539 it passed to the Crown.   In 1583 Queen Elizabeth granted the reversion to Sir Christopher Hatton.   It passed afterwards to Lord Lumley, and with his estate it descended to his nephew, Henry Lloyd.   Henry Lloyd conveyed it to Benjamin Holford on October 1st, 1638, who in the following December sold it to St. John's College, Oxford, for £380, in whose gift the living still is.   The College register says that it was purchased on such easy terms " by the special care and mediation of Archbishop Laud with same."

The Parish Registers commence in 1538, and contain many entries of great interest.

The following entries among the burials seem to refer to the results of a skirmish which took place in 1643 between the

Royal troops and the Parliamentarians, near Worcester Park, in which the Royal troops were ambushed and defeated and retreated through Cheam.

> A soldier who came sicke to the towne buryed June 19, 1643.
> Another soldier called James Brunwell buryed June 26, 1643.
> A soldier called Mattes the Polonian buryed Oct. 12, 1643.

Early in 1923, while making the excavation for the sewer in Parkside, some large bones were found, presumably those of a horse, about three feet below the surface, and among them a spur. This spur is now in the collection in the Old Cottage, and possibly it belonged to one of these soldiers and was torn off when his wounded horse fell on this spot.

Cheam seems to have escaped the plague of 1665, but suffered severely in those of 1603 and 1645.

In 1603 there are ten burials recorded in the register, five of which are described as having died of the pestilence, but as all the ten died in October, 1603, it looks as if they had all been plague victims.

Again, on August 26th, 1645, is the entry: " A poore woman which died at the stables in the Parke of Nonsuch, by name [*blank*]."

On September 8th, 1645, Mrs. Ursula Poynings, wife of the curate-in-charge, " died of ye pestilence." The register contains an epitaph to her in Latin, the translation of which is " She was a pattern of so great virtue that whilst she lived she was a pleasant companion to every saint. God adorned her with so great a love of piety that leaving the world now on high she worships God."

> Marie Borradel, a maid, died of ye pestilence Sept. 23, buryed same day, 1645.
> Ann Barret, d. to Austin Barret, died of ye pestilence Sept. 20, buried Sept. 21, 1645.
> Henry Poynings, Curate of this Parish. Died of ye pestilence Sept. 23, buried ye same day, 1645.

It looks, therefore, as if the poor woman who died in the stable at Nonsuch had brought the infection to the village, with such terrible consequences to the curate and his family.

Photo by E. Douglas Tribe.

The Rectory, Cheam. (*see* p. 40).

There are two interesting records among the marriages:

Apr. 3 1580—Dominus Johes Baron de Lumley et etiam Elizabetha D'arcie desponsati sut tertio die Aprilis 1580.

Elizabeth D'Arcy was the daughter of Lord D'Arcy of Cliche. The D'Arcys of Cliche were connected with Sutton in the reign of Henry VIII, and in 1632 a Lady D'Arcy was living in Sutton.

July 2, 1800—Sydney Smith, Clerk A.M. of New College, Oxford, and Catherine Ameli Pybus.

This was the famous wit, Sydney Smith, Canon of St. Paul's. Catherine Pybus was the daughter of John Pybus of Cheam House.

Among the marriages for 1782 are:

1782   Aug. 25, John Sanders and Mary Smith.
       Sept. 23, James Taylor and Mary Smith.
Mr. Fleming by mistake has inserted the name of Mary Smith as married to James Taylor instead of Sarah Ataway, as will evidently appear by referring to the part of ye register where ye Banns are inserted.—H. Peach, Rector.

Apparently the marriage of September 23rd was solemnised by Mr. Fleming, and in absence of mind he entered the name of the bride of the wedding of August 25th, which is just above it, instead of the correct one, Sarah Ataway.

In 1783 and 1784 no marriages are recorded, though the average number was about four a year, so it looks as if the registers had been carelessly kept at that time.

In the eighteenth century there are many burial entries, to which a note is appended, that the certificate that the body was wrapped in " woolen " was not produced at the time of burial, and that the fact had been reported to the proper authority.

This is the inventory of the goods and ornaments of the Church that was made in 1552 by the order of King Edward VI:

CHEYHAM. The Inventory indentyd of all the goodes and ornamentes purteynyng to the Churches of Chayham in the Countye of Surrey made the vj yere of the reign of our sovereign Lord Kyng Edward the vj by Humfrey Wade and Thomas Saunder parishioners and sidesmen there sworn to present the same as hereafter folowyth:

First ij chalyces of sylver whereof one is gylt and the other parcell gylt. ij leaden crewettes. vjj aulter clothes. one front cloth for an alter of satten of Bridges. iiij fronte clothes for aulters steyned. A sepulcre cloth steyned. An old vestment of sylke and gold. ij vestmentes of readd chamlett. One of readd damaske. One of black Worsted. ij old vestments. vij albes to ye seyd vestmentes porteynyng. A cope of whyte damaske. iiij old copes dornyx. ij corporace copes with corporaces. vj towells. iij surpleses. iij clothes to hang about the sacrament. A cross of copper and gylt. A streamer cloth of sylke. A canopy of Chamlet. ij herseclothes of sarconet. iiij belles in the steple. A little bell called the sanctus bell. iij chestes. A hand bell. A lyttell bell in the chauncell. ij candlestyckes for ye aulter of latten. A cloth steyned to hang upon the roode. A tyble with the boke of servys. A paraphrase of Erasmus. ij salters bokes.

Md. That Randolph Goldsmyth and Robert Orgle were churchwardens in the first yere of the reign of our sovereign lord the King that nowe is. These parcelles of goodes under wrytten purteynyng to the seyd churche of Chayham were sold sense the first yere of the reign of our seid sovereign Lord King as hereafter foloyth:

First one chalyce of sylver. A sylver pax. ij sylver crewettes.

Md. That these parcelles were sold in the moneth of October in the iiij yere of the reign of our seid sovereign Lord the Kynges reign to one — Metcalf of London goldsmyth for iiijli. xvj$s$. by William Carpenter and John Smellyng then churchwardens and by the consent of the whole parish.

A pix of latten. iiij herse candle stycks of latten. xxiiijli. bosses of latten for the rode loft. ij candelsticks of latten for the aulter. a bason and a yewre of latten. a holy water pott of latten. a pascall candlestick of latten.

Md. That all these parcelles last remembryd were sold by the seyd churchewardens and by consent of the hoole parish the vj day of June in the said iiij yere of the reign of our seid sovereign Lord the Kyng to one Thomas Taxsted of London for xxxij$s$. ij$d$. all which sommes of monye were delyveryd and was in the kepyng of the seyd churchewardens and dyd amounte to the sume of vjli. viij$s$. ij$d$. off the seyd which sume of vjli. viij$s$. ij$d$. there was by the consent of the hoole parish gyven to the poore men of the seid parish and employed to the reparacions to shynglyng to glasyng and other necessaries about the seid churche lvj$s$. viij$d$. as itt doth appeare in the accompts thereof made

Photo by W. Sergeant.

Old Cottage, Cheam, before removal.

and also there was lost by the falle of monye of the said somme of vj*li*. viij*s*. ij*d*. the summe of vij*s*. iiij*d*. and the residue of the same some of vj*li*. viij*s*. ij*d*. whiche ys xiij*s*. ij*d*. remanyth nowe in the seid churche box to the use if the same churche.

Thomas Saunder } Sidesmen
Richard Wright   }

John Goldsmith   } Churchewardens.
Richard Gawen   }

Sir Richard Robynson curate 3rd year of Edward **VI.**

A further inventory was made in 1553 :

CHEHAM.

Wardeyns—John Stynte, Thomas Matthew. Delivered unto the wardens ther the xxvj day of Maye anno regni regnis Edwardi Sexti septimo by Sir Thomas Car- warden, Sir Thomas Saunder Knight John Scott Nicholas Leigh and William Saunder esquoirs commissioners of our soveraing Lord the King among others within the Countey of Surrey for the sale of Church goodes these parcelles here after ensuing.

Imprimis a challyce of sylver poz. xij oz. Item ij alter clothes one Bridges satin an other of bawdekyn and a cope of dornix for the communion table.

Also remaining in their charge to the Kynges use foure belles and a saunce bell and ij other little belles.

Received to the Kinges use a challyce sylver and gilt poz xiij oz.

Sales. One stremor of grene sarcenet iij*s*. vj*d*. One painted cloth sold for xix*d*. Brass poz viiij*lb*. xvj*d*. One old stayned cloth xiij*d*. One Crosse cloth xxij*d*. Copper gilt poz iij*lb*. xviij*d*. One painted cloth ij*s*. vj*d*. Received in redy money xiiij*s*. ij*d*. One sarcenet curten ij*s*. iiij*d*. One cope white damask sold for xxj*d*. iij vestementes sold for xiij*s*. iiij*d*. iiij vestementes sold for x*s*. viij*d*. Two copes old silk iij*s*. vj*d*. Two old aulter clothes iij*s*. vj*d*.

Summa iiij*li*. xxij*d*.

In Cheam there are now (in 1936), besides the Parish Church of St. Dunstan, St. John the Baptist, Belmont, erected in 1914; St. Philip's, Worcester Park, in 1876; and St. Alban's in Elm- brook Park Road, in 1930. Another church, St. Oswald's, is shortly to be built to serve a district on which about 1,600 houses have been built recently, on what, until about two years ago, was Messrs. Brock's firework factory. This great addition of population to the parish (the 1,600 houses will accommodate more than 6,000 people) means that they will have to be provided with churches, schools, and other amenities. The new church of St. Oswald's is about to be built in this district as a daughter church to St. Dunstan's. There are also a Baptist Chapel in the Malden Road, built on what was formerly the angle of the garden of West Cheam Manor House, and St. Andrew's Presbyterian Church of England in Northey Avenue.

THE VILLAGE POND was next to the Rectory stables, half surrounded by a brick wall which still remains, where the Institute stands, but was filled in many years ago.

THE POUND, an enclosure bordered by wooden railings, was on the site of the garden of the cottage next to the Institute.

THE RECTORY. The present Rectory is very old, and was probably built about 350 years ago—roughly speaking about 1575—and has been very little altered since Stuart times. It was built either for Anthony Watson, who was rector from 1581 to 1605, or for Sir John Wyrley, the rector immediately before him. On the outside of the dining-room chimney was an inscription which referred to Bishop Watson, but it has now disappeared.

The south-west angle of the house, containing the dining-room, is the oldest part. This part is constructed of timber framing, probably filled in with "rye-dough," but at some later date has been faced with tiles made of the size and colour of bricks to match the other work. The rest of the building is of Stuart and Queen Anne additions.

The old pumping-house in the Rectory garden is nearly as old as the house itself.

A much older house next to the church, and now made into two cottages, is supposed to have been the original Rectory. The ceilings of its rooms have massive beams, and originally it has been built with a large inglenook. It had a very good brick chimney until recently, but this has now been rebuilt and its character quite lost.

THE OLD COTTAGE AND BREWERY. At the NW. corner of the junction of Cheam Road and Malden Road stood a large and picturesque building, pulled down in 1922 for the widening of the road, which had been a brewery since the twelfth century.

The water for the brewery was obtained from a deep well—now filled up—which yielded very good water. Adjoining the brewery and forming part of it was a small sixteenth-century cottage.

Next to this was a fine cottage dating from about 1500. The Epsom Rural Council bought this cottage, and as it was in the way of the widening of Malden Road it was moved to a new site a little further up the road. The building was all framed in oak put together with oak pins, and panels filled in with " rye-dough," *i.e.*, clay mixed up with rye straw. This rye-dough was perfectly preserved, the rye straws being as fresh as if newly cut. The fault of the building had been, as in the case of most of these old framed wooden houses, that the oak had been used freshly cut and unseasoned, and it had shrunk away from the rye-dough filling, and to make the building water-tight it had all been boarded outside. When the building was removed it was found that, with the exception of the sill, three or four rafters, and one angle post, which had been charred by a fire that must have occurred in the house at some unknown period, all the timbers were absolutely sound, and could all be pinned together again, and in many cases the old pins were used for this. The panels are now filled in with reinforced concrete instead of the " rye-dough." The old tiles were re-used as far as possible, about half having to be made up of new tiles. The house was erected between 1480 and 1520, the lean-to at the side having been added at a later date. In the original house the door was on the south side, near the road, the marks of the staple for the bolt and the mortise for the door frame being still visible. Originally there was no glass in the windows, but there were sliding wooden shutters and triangular wood bars in front. The grooves for thsee shutters are now used for sliding glass casements, and new wood bars have been replaced in the old mortise holes. It was found that many of the timbers had been used before they were adapted for this house, and it is suggested that possibly the house may have been removed from Cuddington when Henry VIII pulled down that village to clear the site for Nonsuch Palace. Early in the nineteenth century the house was used as an office for the brewery, and at that time half of the upper floor was cut away and the window on the north side was inserted. The original stairs appear to have been near where the fireplace now is, but this was removed, probably when the lean-to was built, because one of the posts of the lean-to has mortise holes in it that look as if it had been used as the newel of the staircase. Before the building was removed it had a barge-board, but drawings dating from about 1830 do not show any barge-board, so this was omitted when it was re-erected. The Society for the Preservation of Ancient Buildings called the attention of the Epsom Rural Council to the importance of preserving this fine example of the type of early sixteenth-century cottage, and the Council removed it and adapted it for the use of the Cheam Parish Council offices, a purpose for which it was well suited.

The author was appointed by the S.P.A.B. to represent them during the removal. Saving this old cottage has had the effect of setting a standard for the modern buildings in the rebuilding of the centre of Cheam—a standard which has been well maintained by the Onyx Property Investment Co., who have developed this portion of the village, and if this start is only maintained it should result in Cheam becoming one of the prettiest districts near London in its modern form, as it was in the ages that have passed.

A case has been put up in the cottage to preserve all objects of interest that may be found to illustrate the history of the parish, and it contains a complete set of the types of mediæval pottery found in Parkside, and many other objects of interest. It is hoped that all other objects of historical interest found in the parish will be placed there, and thus form the nucleus of a local museum.

WHITEHALL. At the corner of Malden Road and Park Lane stands a fine three-gabled house, now known as Whitehall. The former name of the house was " The Council House." Tradition says that Queen Elizabeth was out hunting one day, when some important despatches were brought to her, and she went into the nearest house, which happened to be Whitehall, and held a council there. The modern name, " Whitehall," was given to it about the time of Charles I, at which time some court official inhabited it and gave it this name after the Palace of Whitehall. Possibly this may have been the Edmund Barrett, Sergeant of the Wine Cellar to King Charles I, who died in Cheam in 1631, to whose memory there is a tablet in the Lumley Chapel.

Photo by C. J. Marshall.

Old Cottage, Cheam, after removal.

The house was built, probably as a farmhouse, in the middle of the sixteenth century. At that time it was a two-storey house with rooms in the roof, and overhung at the back in the same way as it overhangs in the front. It had no porch, and probably the staircase was an outside one. Later in the sixteenth century the porch and the beautiful newel staircase were added. About the time of Charles II a large room, now the drawing-room, was added at the back, with rooms over. This addition was probably made when the school was established there by Mr. Aldrich, and a number of boys were sent to the school from

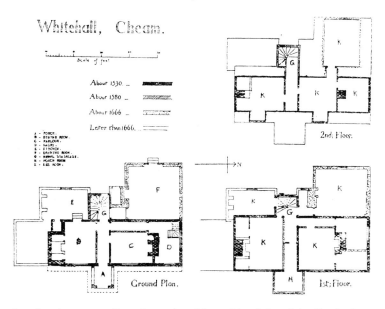

Whitehall, Cheam.

Scale of feet

About 1530 —
About 1580 —
About 1666 —
Later than 1666 —

A - PORCH.
B - DINING ROOM.
C - PARLOUR.
D - DAIRY.
E - KITCHEN.
F - DRAWING ROOM.
G - NEWEL STAIRCASE.
H - PORCH ROOM.
I - BED ROOM.

2nd Floor.

N

F

E

G

B

C

D

A

Ground Plan.

K

K

G

K

K

H

1st Floor.

London to escape the plague in 1665. At a later date the ingle-nooks were closed up and some kitchens and passages added. The house appears to have been inhabited by people who favoured the Royalist cause. In the roof is a room which has a door made out of old planks. On this is written vertically (in Old English characters) the word " Remember," which was the last word of Charles I, and also the letters " D.O.M.," which is the sign of dedication. There is a cellar which at one time must have been much larger, partly built of chalk blocks and partly of bricks. In the dairy is a niche, which it is thought might have been an aumbry in connection with an altar, in which case the dairy must at one time have been used as a chapel. However, this recess is just at the back of a fireplace, and would be a very suitable place for the salt box, so possibly it may have served for this prosaic but useful purpose. The house is constructed of oak framing filled in with "rye-dough," *i.e.*, tempered clay mixed with rye straw, but as in the case of the cottage, the timber had shrunk, and to keep the wet from coming in between the timbers and the "rye-dough" filling, part of the house has been covered over with cement and part is covered with boarding. In the room over the porch some of the original framing and "rye-dough" filling can be seen. A few of the casements are original, with their original casement fasteners.

In 1639 the house was in the possession of Bartholomew Fromond, of East Cheam Manor, and it descended to Richard and Mary Walmisley, and then to their daughter, Catherine, Lady Stourton. Lady Stourton left the house to her son, Lord Petre, who in 1785 sold it to Mr. James Killick, who had at that time been tenant of the house for many years. The house is now in the possession of Mr. Killick's descendants, the Misses Muller.

A story told about the cellar under Whitehall is that about 1750 a bricklayer, repairing the floor of the wash-house, found a vault arched over, and in it was an iron chest. He carried the chest away, telling the owner that there was nothing in it; but from being a poor man he suddenly became wealthy and bought houses in Sutton. This bricklayer died about 1803.

In the roof of Whitehall is an enclosed space that is inaccessible, and it was thought that it was a secret hiding chamber. However, as the enclosing partitions are of hair plaster, it appears to be modern and was probably put up to square out the room.

There are several filled-up Tudor windows that can be seen from the outside of the house, which were probably filled up to avoid window tax.

Next to Whitehall is Laurel Cottage. This is a timber-framed building, boarded on the outside, plastered inside. Running through the centre of the house is a wall of squared chalk blocks, evidently belonging to a former building, but with two doorways knocked through it when the house was altered. The house probably consisted first of two sheds, one built on each side of

Whitehall, Cheam (front).

Photographs by J. W. S. Burmester.

Whitehall, Cheam (back).

the wall. Eventually these two sheds were connected with doors through the chalk wall, and two staircases were put in as there is not height enough for access between the two buildings on the upper floor. The front door at first was on the north side, but at a later period the main staircase was made towards Malden Road. The main framing consists of oak beams ten inches square.

POND HILL COTTAGE was originally a farm-house, and the dairy next door is believed to have been part of the same farm. Pond Hill Cottage has been much enlarged, having a big drawing-room and an extra storey added during the last forty years.

Below Willow Place was a one-storied building divided into four cottages. This was the original Alms Houses for which John Hockon was paid 2/10 for mending the " Tillen " in 1746. This building was called Griffen Row, and had long ceased to be Alms Houses before it was pulled down many years ago.

CHEAM SCHOOL. There was a school in Cheam in 1600, which was held in the belfry of the old church; but it is uncertain whether that school was a parish or a private one, or who was its first headmaster. Certainly many things point to its having been a private school.

The school ceased to be when Mr. George Aldrich brought his school from London during the year of the Great Plague, in 1665. It has been suggested that Aldrich merely took over an already existing school, but the local tradition that it was a London school escaping from the plague to the healthy air of Cheam is too strong to be disregarded. It is probable that the new school absorbed the old and both merged into one.

From surmise we now pass to certainty. Mr. George Aldrich, a non-conformist minister, took the old wooden house known as Whitehall, which is still standing in the village, and there kept his school for some reason or other " as being out of observation." The school was originally kept in the underground vault which stood in the gardens behind the wooden cottages next to Laurel Cottage, which was then part of the gardens of Whitehall. This vault was cut out of the sandstone and was 25 ft. long, 14 ft. broad, and 11 ft. high, and a broad flight of twenty-three steps led down to it. It was used for many purposes before and since the time it was a boys' class-room. The legend was that, in the time of Queen Mary, Protestants gathered there to read the Bible, while later on harassed Roman Catholics said Mass there. Unfortunately, some years ago the roof collapsed in heavy rains and it has now been filled in.

Aldrich is buried in Cheam. " To the Memory of George Aldrich, Native of London," his monument records, with a long Latin inscription. He died in 1685, and during his time the school flourished, many people sending their children to him. His will, dated 16th January, 1685, leaves the lease of Whitehall to his third wife, who survived him eleven years. He leaves to his son, George, " All my books in my study next to my bedchamber, and all my books in my study in the school . . . . but if he prove not a scholar then I will that these my said books be sold or otherwise disposed of." To his daughter, Jane, he bequeaths " My Pendelum Clocke standing in the little parlour, made by Mr. Trippett of Kingston . . . . also my Ebony Cabbinett and the case of drawers that it stands upon." To his son, Valentine, " My Wainscott chest of Drawers and my pendolin clock that stand by it in my bedchamber." He leaves property in the Poultry, in London, and a house in Whitechapel, " which I hold by lease of the Dean of St. Paul's." He wishes to be " interred in the Parish Church at Cheame . . . . my funeral to be with decent frugality."

It is uncertain who continued the school for the next five years after Aldrich's death in 1685; but that it did continue there is no doubt. In Aldrich's time the drawing-room at White-hall, and the room above it, were built to accommodate the school, which had grown too big for the vaults. The boys were now living in the house, and it is probable that the school was also held in a one-storey building which stood in the kitchen garden of Cheam House and in later days was used as a fruit room. The house is now in the Malden Road, opposite Parkside. It has had another storey put on it, and is now used as a dwelling-house and is called Necton. The date 1775 has been recently placed over the door, but it is certainly an older building than that. Among the pupils at this time was Charles Davenant (afterwards writer, LL.D. and M.P.), son of Sir William Davenant, the Poet Laureate. He went to Oxford in 1671, so was probably at Cheam until that date.

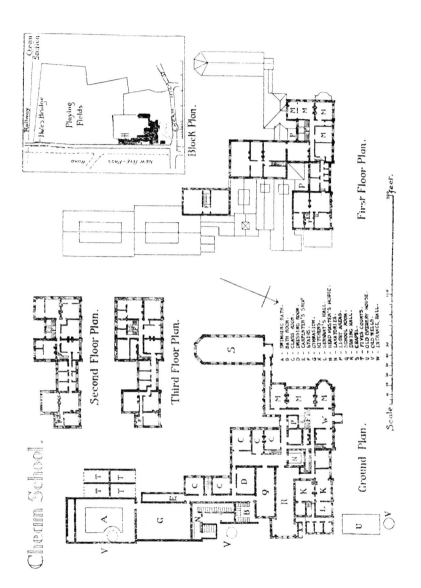

Cheam School.

Block Plan.

Railway
Pixes Bridge
Playing
Fields
New Rye-Pass
Road
Ouem
Station

First Floor Plan.

Second Floor Plan.

Third Floor Plan.

Ground Plan.

A - SWIMMING BATH.
B - BATH ROOM.
C - CLASS ROOM.
D - DRESSING ROOM.
E - CARPENTER'S SHOP.
F - STAIRS.
G - GYMNASIUM.
G X - KITCHENS.
L - SERVANT'S HALL.
M - HEAD MASTER'S HOUSE.
N - LAVATORIES.
P - LIGHT AREAS.
Q - SCHOOL ROOM.
R - DINING HALL.
S - CHAPEL.
T - FIVES COURTS.
U - OLD BREWERY HOUSE.
V - OLD WELLS.
W - ENTRANCE HALL.

Scale of feet.

Dr. Daniel Sanxay came to Cheam in 1690, and probably he lived at Whitehall, though this is rather uncertain. He built the present Cheam School on the Cheam Road in 1719 on a ninety-nine years' lease, which expired in 1818. He was the author of a book entitled *Lexicon Aristophanicum.*

Dr. Sanxay was buried in Cheam May 28th, 1740, and was succeeded at the school by his son, James Sanxay, who resigned when he was made rector of Sutton. This must have been between August, 1753, and July, 1755, as the first year records the baptism of a Sanxay daughter, and the last that of a Gilpin son. So the Rev. William Gilpin, who was the next headmaster, must have come to Cheam about 1754.

Mr. Gilpin was immortalized as "Dr. Syntax." He was the author of many books—among others a *Life of Bernard Gilpin* (of whom he was a collateral descendant), and biographies of Wycliffe, Cobham, Huss, Cranmer, etc., which were all written at Cheam. His more famous book, *Forest Scenery*, was written at Boldre. He made changes in the routine of the school. " For corporal punishment he substituted imprisonment with excise imposed by a jury of boys, and fines which were spent on the school library and five courts, and on the poor." " He encouraged gardening among the boys " and planted four noted elm trees on the lawn of Cheam School. He was appointed rector of Boldre in 1777 and left the school to his son William.

Cheam School now became famous all over England. Fanny Burney, afterwards Madame D'Arbley, the authoress of *Evelina*, writes in her diary on December 14th, 1785, reporting a conversation at Windsor Castle :

> After this Mrs. Delaney mentioned Madame de la Fite and her son.
> The Queen said: " He is a pretty little boy; when he goes to school it will do him good."
> " Where will she send him ? " asked the King.
> The Queen, looking at me with a smile, answered: " To the school where Mr. Lock puts his sons, I know."
> " Where is that ? " asked the King.
> " Now I do not know. Where is it, Miss Burney ? "
> " At Cheam, ma'am."
> " Oh, at young Gilpin's," cried the King. " Is it near Mr. Lock's ? "
> " Yes, Sir, within six miles, I believe."

CHEAM SCHOOL.

Front in 1834.
Back in 1834.

Front in 1935.
Back in 1935.

Henry Addington, afterwards Viscount Sidmouth, was one of Mr. Gilpin's pupils, and when he was Prime Minister in 1802 he visited Cheam and dined with the boys in what was afterwards the entrance hall, but which then was the dining-room.

William Gilpin, the son, died in December, 1809, but before then the school had been taken over by Mr. James Wilding, who was also curate of Cheam.

In Mr. Gilpin's obituary notice in the *Gentleman's Magazine* for December, 1809, it states:

> In the time of the Rev. Mr. Gilpin the numbers of scholars usually exceeded 80, but by the increase of his son's family, who necessarily occupied the space allotted for the pupils' accommodation, the number rarely exceeded 60 from 1796 to 1804. Since Mr. Gilpin's leaving Cheam the establishment has been transferred to the Rev. J. Wilding from Cambridge, who has called in the assistance of the Rev. Mr. Wilson as a partner. These gentlemen are eminently qualified to support the character invariably attached to the Semenary."

The new headmasters had evidently taken the school before July, 1809, as the *Gentleman's Magazine* for that date remarks:

> Rev. J. Wilson, of Cheam School, announced his intention of publishing a series of letters as an Introduction to Bishop Butler's *Analogy of Natural and Revealed Religion.*

Dr. Wilding was succeeded by Dr. Charles Mayo. He was a great believer in the Pestalozzian System, and before coming to Cheam he went to Yverdon in Switzerland and worked in Henry Pestalozzi's school as English Chaplain. He remained there for three years, and after having had a school at Epsom for about four years, he came to Cheam in 1826. He wrote *Memoirs of Pestalozzi* and many other books while he was at Cheam.

His sister, Miss Elizabeth Mayo, joined her brother, first at Epsom, and then at Cheam, where she remained till 1834. She helped him in instructing the boys in his method. A book describing the principles of this system was printed for the school at Cheam and has now become very scarce. There is a copy in the British Museum Library. During her time at Cheam Miss Mayo wrote *Lessons on Objects* in 1831, and *Lessons on Shells* in 1832.

Cheam School was now most famous and was always full. As soon as a child was born his name was put down for Cheam, as to-day boys' names are put down for public schools.

At the end of 1845 Dr. Mayo's health began to fail, and his brother-in-law, Mr. Shepheard, offered to come and be one of the masters and take over the headmastership by degrees. This he did in February, 1846, when the boys came back to school. Dr. Mayo died a month later. He is buried in Cheam churchyard. The original grave was designed by Sir Charles Barry, who built the Houses of Parliament, but as the stone was the same as that used in the Houses of Parliament, it was not very durable, and it was copied later, exactly, in permanent stone, and the present grave is the copy. On it is inscribed the collect from the burial service and above it the emblems of the Resurrection—the caterpillar, the chrysalis, and the butterfly. In the same grave lies the little Earl of Carrick, who died as a boy at the school.

Mr. Shepheard kept the school on, but although he was a very clever man, he was not a born schoolmaster, and the school went down. He finally sold it to Mr. R. S. Tabor in 1855.

Mr. Tabor decided only to have boys from 8 to 14 years old, and weeded out the elder boys, some of whom were over 20 years of age. He added the extra storey and the porch which bears his initials, as well as many other improvements. The chapel was built in 1867; before that the boys had always occupied a side gallery in old Cheam Church.

The record of the school became exceedingly high, and among the pupils were the Rt. Hon. Hugh Childers, a minister under Gladstone; Vernon Lushington, son of the famous Judge; Capt. George Norman, who was killed in the Indian Mutiny; Charles Lloyd-Norman, a noted cricketer; Dr. Edward Freshfield; the Duke of Marlborough; Lord Randolph Churchill; Lord Durham and his brother, Admiral Sir Hedworth Lampton; Lord Hardinge of Penshurst; Lord Aberdeen; General Sir Ian Hamilton, and many more.

Mr. A. S. Tabor came to be master in 1875 and succeeded his father as headmaster in 1890. He was headmaster for thirty years, and left Cheam in 1920, when he was succeeded by the Rev. H. M. S. Taylor. Mr. Taylor carried on the school at Cheam until 1934, when, on account of so many houses having been

Photo by *J. W. S. Burmester.*

Cheam School, Staircase.

built in the neighbourhood, he decided to remove it further into the country, and accordingly the school has been removed to Beenham Court, near Newbury, Berks.

The building had been very substantially built and it had a very fine staircase, and it seemed a pity that the buildings could not have been kept and adapted to some other purpose. The beautiful playing fields, with turf that had been kept in perfect condition for very many years, are all cut up and destroyed.

At the outbreak of war hundreds of old boys joined the Colours, or were already serving in the Navy and Army: 563 names have been collected, but there were probably more. 143 were mentioned in dispatches; one gained the V.C.; twenty-six the Military Cross; fifty the D.S.O., and twenty gained other decorations.

There were 126 names recorded on the beautiful carved War Memorial in the School Chapel, which was unveiled in July, 1923, by the Marquis of Milford Haven, himself an old Cheam boy.

The inscription was as follows:

> Trained in this school to play the game without self-seeking and to face life without fear or boasting, those whose names are inscribed on this memorial faced death with courage and simplicity and are for ever part of the Glory of England.

CHEAM HIGH STREET.

The greater part of Cheam High Street has been pulled down owing to the widening of the roadway. One old house that has gone is Vine Cottage, which stood on the right coming from Sutton entering Cheam village.

On the left was an interesting house, now destroyed. The back portion was of Tudor work, built of squared chalk blocks and flint squares built as chequer-work. On the front of this was a timber building dating from about the time of William and Mary.

A well about seventy-eight feet deep was found close to the roadway of the High Street.

Opposite this house on the right (north) side of the High Street is a building that at one time must have been a very fine house. The ground floor on the side next the High Street is built of chequer-work of squared blocks of chalk alternating with flint-work squares. The remainder of the house is oak-framed and filled in with "rye-dough," or, where this has got out of repair, with brickwork. It has been a large house with inglenooks, but its history is unknown. At some time it has been cut up into three tenements, and though it is now in one

OLD COTTAGE ON SOUTH SIDE OF HIGH STREET, CHEAM, SURREY.   PULLED DOWN IN 1934.

S.W. View from back garden: showing chalk block, flint, and brickwork probably Tudor work.
The front part was added later, and is said to have been built in the time of William and Mary.

occupation the three staircases and entrances remain.

On the west side of this house is the house (now a fish shop) that in the sixteenth century was built over the site of the thirteenth-century pottery kiln. It was a timber-framed building, having the upper floor projecting over the lower, both at the front and back. In the middle of last century the front was rebuilt in brick, and more recently the ground floor back wall has been rebuilt on the line of the upper storey. The back part of the upper storey is thus the original sixteenth-century work,

CHEAM.

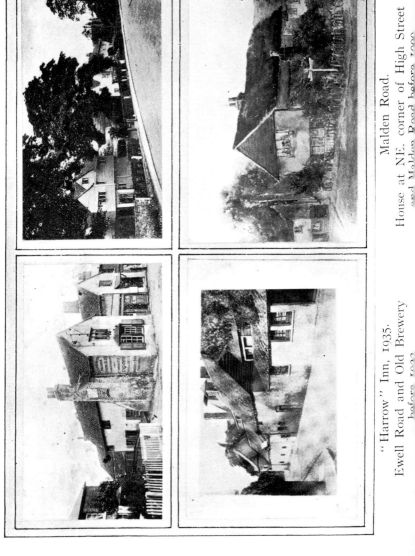

"Harrow" Inn, 1935.

Ewell Road and Old Brewery before 1922.

Malden Road.

House at N.E. corner of High Street and Malden Road before 1922.

but the timber and "rye-dough" panels have been covered with weather-boarding, which was probably done in the late eighteenth century.

It would almost appear as if these two houses had some connection with each other, and perhaps formed one block of buildings. At any rate this part of the High Street must have been very tortuous and steep, for in coaching days the coaches did not attempt to come down the High Street, but if they were coming from the Sutton direction they turned round by the White House into Park Road (then Red Lion Street), went down Park Lane, and so back into the main road by Cheam Park.

Similar chequer-work of squared blocks of chalk and flints, probably Tudor, can be seen in the remains of the stables of West Cheam Manor House, opposite Church Farm House.

THE HARROW INN shares with the Red Lion the distinction of being the oldest inn in Cheam. It is about 350 years old. More than a century ago there was a brewery behind the Harrow, where the innkeeper brewed his own ale. In the days of the prize fights on Banstead Downs many of the sportsmen who came to see them put up at the Harrow. The sign hanging over the High Street was a very fine piece of work. The inn has recently been rebuilt.

THE PLOUGH INN has now been removed to a new site in Gander Green Lane, and the old building has been pulled down. Originally the Plough Inn was in an old house that stood on the north side of the High Street, which was pulled down about 1900. Behind this old house stood Cheam Square, a group of small houses, some of which are known from drawings, but all traces of which have now vanished. Next to this old house in the Malden Road was a small group of wooden cottages known as Acha Cottages, now pulled down, but there is no record of what the name Acha referred to.

There was an old inn called the "Cock" which stood in Park Lane, opposite the gates of Cheam Park, an old engraving of which is now in the Borough Offices. The most southerly house in Park Lane may have been this inn.

It may be mentioned here that till comparatively recent years football was played through the village on Shrove Tuesday.

It was an old custom which is sometimes to be met with in other parts of England.

On the 1st of May the school children used to come round to the various houses bringing garlands and singing songs, and expected to be rewarded with pennies and sweets, and this custom was kept up until about 1910.

THE HOUSES IN PARK ROAD (starting from the corner of Malden Road) :

WHITE LODGE. This is a square white house which stands at the corner of Park Road, opposite to Whitehall. It was built in 1740. It may have been built by Dr. Sanxay, of Cheam School, as he at one time owned the land.

The house, part of which is panelled, belonged to a family named Joy in the early days of the nineteenth century. One of them, the then owner, was a great sportsman. One day, after a coursing match on Banstead Downs, George IV, then Prince Regent, came back with him to luncheon at the White Lodge. The dinner service used on that occasion has been carefully preserved and is now in the possession of an old Cheam resident.

BAY COTTAGE. It is said that this house, and THE CABIN next door, were practically built out of the materials from the old Palace of Nonsuch. The front door, with its fan-light, is supposed to have been designed by Adams, but this is not certain and would be of later date than Nonsuch.

The cottages between Bay Cottage and the Red Lion date back to the days of Henry VIII, and in the last, No. 7, there is an unusually broad staircase for the size of the house.

THE RED LION. This is a very old building, going back at least 350 years. The red brick front was added some years ago, covering the old wooden front with its two bow windows. One of the rooms at the back is panelled. Not so very long ago the old well was in daily use.

The story goes that a murder was committed at the Red Lion more than a hundred years ago, and a description of it is said to have appeared in a book published about 1850.

According to the old rate book, the half-yearly meetings of the Vestry were held in the Red Lion, and as the first item of expenditure in each half year is " disbursements at meeting of

MALDEN ROAD, CHEAM.

Park Lane.
Malden Road about 1922.

"White Lodge" and Parochial Rooms.
Malden Road about 1900.

the Vestry at the Red Lion," the business appears to have been done under pleasant conditions at the expense of the ratepayers.

CHURCH FARM HOUSE lies to the east of the church, and the dining-room appears to be part of the original structure, built with timber posts filled in with brickwork, and with oak beams showing in the ceiling, and may be Tudor. A few years ago extra imitation posts and beams were put in so that it is now difficult to trace the original structure. A wing on the west side was added in early Georgian times, and a drawing-room and hall in early Victorian times. The house is now used as a preparatory school for boys. The last farmer who lived there and cultivated Church Farm, about twenty-five years ago, was Mr. Hales. Part of the farm was on the south side of the railway, and there was a narrow occupation bridge giving communication between the two parts of the farm, and this was known as Hales' Bridge. It occupied the position of the present bridge over the railway carrying the by-pass road, and is still known as " Hales' Bridge." This bridge was on the line of an old track shown in Roche's map of Surrey, which is now Manor Road, and ran from Burdon Lane till it joined Love Lane.

Near Church Farm House is part of the old wall of West Cheam Manor on the side of the lane leading from the church-yard to Church Road, very well built of squared chalk blocks, still in excellent condition.

STAFFORD HOUSE. This is an old house which has been added to considerably. It was originally a square white house, much the same as Cheam Cottage next door, though the latter is an older house. Stafford House was a boys' school about 1830, or even earlier, and was kept by a Mr. Brown, who lived here with his two maiden sisters. The school had no connection with Cheam School, but when Cheam School was full up (and there was generally a long waiting list), Dr. Mayo, then headmaster, used to recommend would-be pupils' parents to this school with the words: " Perhaps my friend, Mr. Brown, would take him."

Mr. Brown's pupils were of all ages, from men of twenty to quite little boys. Among them was George W. Thornbury (1828–1871), a writer and friend of Charles Dickens, for whom he wrote in *Household Words* and *All the Year Round*. He

proved " one of Charles Dickens' most valuable contributors "
(*Dickens' Letters*, II, 170; III, 239). He also wrote the first
two volumes of *Old and New London*, but died before its completion. He was a nephew by marriage of the Rev. Barton
Bouchier, curate of Cheam, who lived next door and apparently
taught in this school, as the *Dictionary of National Biography*
states Thornbury was educated at Cheam by " Barton Bouchier,
who was husband of his father's sister, Mary."

After Mr. Brown and the school left, the house was taken
by a Mrs. Stafford, who called it Stafford Cottage, after herself.
The title was later raised to Stafford House, when the big
drawing-room and billiard-room were added, about fifty-five
years ago.

CHEAM COTTAGE. The date of this house is uncertain, but
the title deeds are dated 1672. One of its chief inhabitants was
Richard Wyatt, who came to Cheam about 1729. His name
appears for years in the Cheam rate book. He did a great deal
for the house, adding the bow-windows in the drawing-room
and dining-room (the one to the left of the front door was added
in 1894), the bookshelves which line the morning-room, and
various improvements. He states in his will: " the purchase
whereof and the beautifying new buildings and repairing the
same hath cost me Two Thousand Pounds."

He died in 1753, and his wife, Susanna, lived here as a widow
for twenty years.

The house passed through other tenants to Mr. Robert
Sanxay, the son of Dr. Sanxay of Cheam School. He died here
in 1780.

Among its more modern inhabitants was the Rev. Barton
Bouchier, curate-in-charge of Cheam, who took pupils and
apparently taught in the school next door. Probably George
Thornbury, his nephew, lived in this house, though he went
to Mr. Brown's school.

Mr. Bouchier wrote a book entitled *My Parish*, or *The Country
Parson's Visit to his Poor*, which was published in 1856, and
is dated from Cheam Cottage.

THE WHITE HOUSE. This is the last house in Park Road,
and stands at the corner of Cheam Road. It is not known when
the house was built, but it must have been standing in the
seventeenth century.

The first known inhabitants were Samuel Peirson, who died 1699, and his wife Ann. They were the founders of the Peirson Charity, in which they made a condition that the owner of their house was always to be one of the Trustees of this Charity.

They were followed by the Kempsons. After that there is a gap in the history of the house till 1810, when a family named Penfold were living there, though they probably came to Cheam at a much earlier date.

In those days the front entrance was at the corner of Cheam Road. The original gate was a very handsome wrought iron one, and the piers were—and are still—surmounted by large stone balls. These gates have long since disappeared, and the gateway has been blocked up.

From the Penfolds the house passed into the hands of Mr. Simon Beck, and on his death to his son Ralph. Mr. Ralph considerably altered the house, making the entrance on the other side, adding the drive gate and building extra rooms. When Mr. Antrobus died in 1899 Mr. Beck purchased Lower Cheam House and lived there for a short time. The White House, which was then so named for the first time, was let to various tenants.

During the War the house was a Belgian home from February 1916 to May 1918. Afterwards it became a small hospital for soldiers, and was run by the Cheam V.A.D.'s, Surrey 136, until March 1919.

The beautiful mahogany doors are a great feature of the house.

THE LODGE (Gander Green Lane). When the East Cheam Manor Estate was broken up, about 1785, and the Manor House bought by John Antrobus, a large part of the ground was sold to John Hilbert, Esq., of Wandsworth. His descendants, a family named Tate, lived in the house now called The Lodge, which stands at the beginning of Gander Green Lane, and nearly opposite to Tate Road, which takes its name from the former owners. It is a long red-brick house, standing back from the road, and has an avenue of old chestnut trees leading up to it. The present house has only been built about eighty years, and was originally a farm.

At the corner of Tate Road and Gander Green Lane there stood an old cottage which was pulled down about twenty years ago. A silver Elizabethan coin was found in digging up the ground after the demolition.

CHEAM HALL. There was a much older house on the north side of Tate Road. This house was called Cheam Hall, and it was in this older house that Mrs. Eliza Dutton lived. She was the daughter of Henry and Christian Neal, who belonged to an old Cheam family. Her chief claim to fame is that in trying to make peace between a neighbour and his wife she was murdered on July 13th, 1687. She was a widow, aged 53. It seems somewhat hard that her well-meant efforts should have met with so unkind a response. She is buried in Cheam churchyard with her parents and her son, under a stone tomb to the right of the centre path leading to the church. The following is inscribed on it:

> Here lieth the bodies of Christian, the wife of Henry Neal, of Cheame, who was buried the 29th March, 1664, and the said Henry Neal, who was buried the 29th August, 1664.
>
> Also their daughter, Eliza Dutton, who was murthered the 13th July, 1687, by her neighbour whilst endeavouring to make peace between him and his wife. Aged 53 years.
>
> Here lyes the best of wives, of mothers, friends,
> Whose soul—too good for earth—in Heaven ascends
> With joy and comfort till the day of doome,
> When all her virtuous deeds shall thither come.
> To save her neighbour she has spilt her blood,
> And like her Saviour, died in doing good.
> May that curs'd hand forget itself to feed
> That made its benefactor thus to bleed.
>
> Here lies also the body of Delaval Dutton, her son, who departed this life the 22nd of May, 1689.

This epitaph is attributed to Sir William Davenant, the Poet Laureate, whose son Charles was a pupil at Cheam School; but as Sir William died in 1668 and Mrs. Dutton in 1687 this is an impossibility. It is, however, very likely that Charles Davenant, his son, who was also a writer, heard the story on one of his visits to Cheam, and wrote the epitaph.

About sixty years ago Sir Edmund Antrobus bought the Cheam Hall Farm to complete a ringed fence round the Lower Cheam House Estate, but with the departure of the Antrobus family in 1899 it has again been sold.

CEDAR COTTAGE. On the opposite side of Gander Green Lane

Cheam Park.

Lower Cheam House, 1932 (*see* p. 15).

to the Lodge is Cedar Cottage, which appears to have been built in Georgian times, and has some interesting fireplaces and other features.

CHEAM PARK. This house, which was built in the early days of the nineteenth century, appears to have very little history. It was built by Mr. Archdale Palmer, who was a London tea merchant. He and his wife had lived in London for many years, and there six children had been born to them, none of whom had survived. So for his wife's sake he came to Cheam and built the house about 1820. A daughter was born soon after, who lived to grow up. She married Mr. Wickham, who came to live at Cheam Park. Her descendants owned the property, although they did not live there until Mrs. Bethell bought it some years ago.

It is related of Mr. Palmer that he used to ride up to London every morning. He rode across the park to the further lodge on the Malden Road. This ride took him just about an hour to reach London.

Mr. Palmer gave the site for the Boys' School on the Malden Road, which was built in 1826. All the left-hand side of the Malden Road, from Pond Hill Cottage nearly to Hemmingford Road, was formerly part of the Cheam Park Estate.

This part of Cheam Park (now behind Park Villas and the Boys' School) was let to a Mr. John Fiddyment, who lived in the village, and was used by him for many years as a place for Sunday school treats, etc., for which he catered. Large parties of school children from the East End of London, numbering between 2,000 and 3,000, used to come every day during the summer months. He erected all kinds of amusements, swings, roundabouts, and a long toboggan railway, which latter had an unfortunate habit of breaking down. It was here that the village entertainments for Queen Victoria's Jubilee and Diamond Jubilee were held.

Cheam Park House was let by the Wickhams to several families in turn—the Carrs (Mr. Isaac Carr and his wife are buried in the churchyard); the Durrants; Mr. Souley; Mr. and Mrs. Jacomb (in whose time the billiard-room was added in 1890); and Mr. and Mrs. Bethell. Mr. Bethell was chairman of the Parish Council and did a great work for Cheam until his death in 1908.

There is an interesting row of cottages in Malden Road, near Park Lane, which has the date 1520 on it, but it is not known when this date was put on, or what authority there was for putting it there. These houses and those in the part of Park Lane running from the Malden Road to the gates of Cheam Park, and those on the south side of the part of Park Lane on the east side of Malden Road, now called Park Road, all appear to be about the same date and make an exceedingly picturesque group. They may well be Tudor work.

THE OLD VILLAGE SMITHY, which stood at the corner of Malden Road and Park Lane, was built about 400 years ago, and was kept by members of the Barnes family, some of whom were " iron workers and blake smythes " to Lord Lumley of Cheam and Nonsuch in 1590. The Barnes family apparently held the business from then until the beginning of this century. There is mention of them in 1680 and again in 1720. Some time after that date the last owner, William Barnes, removed the business to the yard of the Harrow Inn. On William Barnes' death his two sons divided. Moses bought an existing smithy situated in the old quarry behind the Railway Hotel, and Henry continued on in the Harrow Yard. Eventually Moses Barnes built a smithy close to the railway bridge over Station Road in 1860. On his death in 1878 his son carried on the business at the same place until his death in 1895. He was succeeded by his son William, who sold the business to Mr. James Winter in 1910 and emigrated to Australia. Mr. Winter sold the business about ten years ago, and the smithy, though still standing, has been put to several other uses, the coming of the motor-car spoiling the business of shoeing horses. This is a good example of how the families in the villages passed on their business from father to son—in this case for about 400 years.

The smithy still stands, and the photograph shows what it was like ten years ago; but now that public buildings can be defaced with advertisements it is no longer a thing of beauty, as the picturesque railway bridge is now a vulgar advertising station. It is a great pity that the Borough Council does not adopt the bye-law to give them control over advertising, and stop the hideous, vulgar advertising on this bridge and other places.

Malden Road, Cheam, in 1834.

The Old Forge, Cheam.

CHEAM HOUSE. This house, which was pulled down about 1922, stood on the west side of Malden Road—the site now occupied by the new shops and the road called Parkside. It was probably built about 1768 by John Pybus, and was a long red-brick house, faced with white stone-work. The original entrance was in Park Lane, nearly opposite the gates of Cheam Park, from which a drive led up to the house. The now existing portion of the Malden Road from the Cross Roads to Park Lane was only a cart track running at the back of Cheam House. With the exception of the cottages in Park Lane, the shops belonging to Mrs. Rowe and Mr. Mould, the old Brewery (now destroyed), and a house which stood at the corner of Park Lane and the Ewell Road, Cheam House and its gardens occupied the whole of the square bordered by the Malden Road, Ewell Road and Park Lane.

John Pybus, its first owner, was born at Dover in 1727. He was a distinguished man, and for twenty-five years filled important posts in India and Ceylon. He was " Chief of Masulipalam, a member of the Council of Madras, and Ambassador to the King of Ceylon, and was the first Englishman received in a public character at that Prince's Court." He married Martha Small, and returned to England in 1768, when he settled in Cheam. He had two sons and six daughters.

One son, Charles, was a Lord of the Admiralty in the Pitt Administration. This son was extremely annoyed when his sister Catherine became engaged to the renowned Sydney Smith, author and wit, and, the biography says, " behaved towards his sister in a very ungraceful manner, and with something of the lofty severity of an indignant parent." But Kitty Pybus went her own way in spite of her brother's objection.

" I was 22," she wrote afterwards, " and my mother said if I chose to forego the comforts and luxuries to which I had been born, I alone was to be the sufferer, and to my ability to decide upon that which best constitute my happiness there could be no more doubt than of my right. She had one wish— that I should be happy. She had long known and loved Sydney, and if to marry him was my resolve, she would not oppose it."

So they were married in Cheam church on July 2nd, 1800, by the rector, Mr. Peach. It is said that during the service, when the bridegroom got to the words " with all my worldly goods I thee endow," he added in a whisper " Six silver tea-spoons, Kitty ! " This was the extent of his possessions.

" His entire fortune," their daughter, Lady Holland, writes long after, " consisted of six small silver teaspoons, which from much wear had become ghosts of their former selves."

A sister of Kitty's, Ann, married in 1774 Brigadier-General Sir Robert Fletcher, Commander-in-Chief of the British Forces on the coast of Coromandel. She died a widow in February, 1791, and according to the inscription in the Lumley Chapel she " was called without a moment's warning from the enjoy-ment of cheerfulness and apparent health into the awful presence of her Creator." Her mother, Mrs. Pybus, gave Lady Fletcher's pearl necklace to Mrs. Sydney Smith. This necklace was said to be the finest ever brought to England. Unfortunately, the Smiths, who were extremely poor, were obliged to sell it.

Following John Pybus' death in 1789, his son John appears to have continued to live at Cheam House. It was during his time that a ball was given there in 1793, and Mr. Killick, of Whitehall (the father of Miss Killick who died in 1914), then a young man, remembered that while they were dancing the news of the execution of Louis XVI of France was brought in.

Robert Percy Smith, more usually known as " Bobus " Smith, bought Cheam House in 1810. He, like his brother Sydney, was an exceedingly witty man. Many of his Latin verses were published by his son in 1850. He was Advocate-General of Bengal, and died in 1845, a fortnight after his brother Sydney. He is buried in Cheam churchyard in a large railed-in tomb on the south side of the Lumley Chapel. His son, Robert Vernon, later became the first Lord Lyveden.

Mrs. Pybus' pet dog, " Nick," was buried in the garden of Cheam House. A wooden monument was erected over the grave with the following verse, composed by Sydney Smith himself:

> Here lies poor Nick, an honest creature,
> Of faithful, gentle, courteous nature;
> A parlour pet, unspoil'd by favour,
> A pattern of good dog behaviour.
> Without a wish, without a dream
> Beyond his home, and friends at Cheam,
> Contentedly through life he trotted
> Along the path that fate allotted;

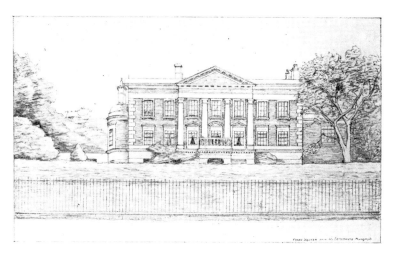

Cheam House from Malden Road.

Cheam House from Park Lane.

Till time, his aged body wearing,
Bereaved him of his sight and hearing,
Then laid him down without a pain,
To sleep, and never wake again !
Reader, dost thy reflection tell
Thou'st lived so wisely and so well ?
If not, go mind thee while thou mayest,
And take example from a beast,
For many a gentleman may pick
A lesson from the life of Nick.

This monument unfortunately disappeared when the house
was pulled down.

Sydney Smith's daughter Saba (a name invented by him
that she might not have two commonplace names) married Sir
Henry Holland, and was famous for the biography of her father
and other works. She was often at Cheam House. She had
the rather odd fancy that she could not sleep in a strange bed,
and when visiting she was in the habit of taking her own bed
with her, strapped on the back of her coach. The late Miss
Killick used to say she had often seen Lady Holland drive past
Whitehall to Cheam House with the bed in attendance at the
back!

When the Malden Road was cut through the gardens of
Cheam House, alterations were made in the house so that the
entrance was from this new road, the original back of the house
thus becoming the front. Evidently about this time the house
at the corner of Ewell Road and Park Lane, which is said to
have been inhabited by a man named Barker, was pulled down,
and the gates, a pair of very handsome wrought iron ones,
were removed to two entrances to the kitchen garden facing
Cheam House on the other side of the Malden Road. These
gates were believed to have come originally from Nonsuch Palace,
though some people say they were brought from West Cheam
Manor House. Unfortunately, like many other things, they
are no longer in Cheam. In 1923 they were bought by a gentleman at Thames Ditton, to be re-erected in the garden of a house
he was building.

Cheam House was bought by Mr. George Wilde, and passed
on his death to his son, Spencer. Mr. Spencer Wilde gave the
land for the Parochial Rooms, and presented the lych gate in
memory of his silver wedding. After his death the house was

let to various tenants, among whom were Mr. H. Bibby and General Lorn Campbell.

Being empty at the outbreak of war in 1914, it was used to accommodate German prisoners, who remained till the armistice.

The house gradually fell into decay, and was pulled down in 1922. At one time it was covered with white plaster, but this was removed some years ago, and the beautiful old brick, with its white facings, brought to light again. In one of the bedrooms was a fine old fireplace. There was supposed to be a ghost who tapped, but its story is unknown. It was under the

A Wrought Iron Gateway from Cheam House, Surrey

tennis courts of Cheam House that, in digging the foundations of some houses in Parkside, the discovery of the mediæval pottery was made in April, 1923.

CHEAM COURT FARM. This house and farm stood at the south-west corner of the Crossways. It was a very picturesque group of buildings, with the old house, the farm-yard, and thirteen barns and cow-houses. The house itself was very interesting. The oldest part was the dining-room, which was part of the old hall, and had a heavy beamed ceiling. The house must have been of not later than early Tudor times, as it was built as a " hall-place," having its fireplace in the middle of the room and being open up to the roof. Later on a large ingle-

Park Road, Cheam, with " Red Lion " (*see* p. 54).

Houses in Malden Road, Cheam, with date 1520 (*see* p. 60).

nook was added, and two floors were put in, making this part of the house three storeys high. In Georgian times, or earlier, some kitchens were added. These were at various levels, with two or three steps from one to the other. On pulling the house down a space was found under one of the floors, about 3' 6" high, enclosed with a pair of open sparred doors. These doors were not visible till found at the demolition, but that part of the house was always pointed out as " the priest's hiding-place." As Cheam seems several times to have been searched for hidden Roman Catholic priests, it may have served for that purpose, but it is most likely that it was originally constructed as a dog kennel. In early Victorian times the drawing-room was built, and

EXTERIOR OF BARN CHURCH, CHEAM.

many alterations were made when the railway came to Cheam in 1845, and Station Road was made, cutting away part of the house.

There was a tradition that there were two underground passages from Cheam Court, one leading to Nonsuch, and the other to the Carews' house at Beddington; and the one to Nonsuch is said to have had a connection to Whitehall, Cheam. However, on pulling the house down, no trace of these underground passages was found. On opening one of the supposed entrances to these passages, it was found to lead to an old well.

In 1929 the house was up for sale for demolition. The rector and churchwardens of Cheam church were at that time

planning to build a new church in Gander Green Lane. In the
Parish Magazine that month appeared an article on a church
at North Sheen that had been built out of some old barns that
had been demolished at Oxted, Surrey. It struck the author
that here were some beautiful barns on the spot, and it would
be a good opportunity to do the same thing at Cheam.
The rector and churchwardens took up the idea, bought
the whole of the buildings that were up for demolition, and

The interior of the Barn Church, Cheam.

appointed the author and Mr. Swan of Oxted (who had been
architect for the North Sheen church) as joint architects for
the new church. They accordingly pulled down the old house
and barns, built the new church out of the materials, and
sold off the materials that were not wanted. They were thus
able to construct a church, at a low cost, that already had a
tradition attached to it, and much of the atmosphere and colour-
ing of age. The nave of the church is constructed from two

"Diver's Ditch" (*see* p. 2).

"Lord Nelson" Inn, London Road,
now part of St. Anthony's Hospital. (*see* p. 69)

of the larger barns, and the aisles are from the cow-sheds. The organ chamber is the front of one of the smaller barns, with Tudor brick coigns from the ingle-nook in the old hall. The Jacobean floor that had been put into the hall now forms the ceiling of the vestry. The font is the font of the 1746 church at Cheam. The demolition and building of the church was carried out by Messrs. Stevenson & Glyde of Cheam, who thoroughly entered into the spirit of the thing and did the building in the mediæval manner without scaffolding, using a movable platform and derricks. The timbers of the barns were in very good condition. All the framing had been pinned together with oak pins, and these were so hard that it was most difficult to get them out. Sometimes they could be knocked out, but if this was impossible, they had to be drilled out, and they broke the very best drills that could be got. The church stands at the corner of Elmbrook Road and Gander Green Lane, and is dedicated to St. Alban.

In the wall of the church a stone has been built in with an inscription, telling where the materials of the church came from, and indicating the spirit in which the church was built :

> This church was built of materials from Cheam Court Farm, one of the farms attached to Nonsuch Palace. These old beams are parts of the barns when Queen Elizabeth was at Nonsuch. The glories of Nonsuch have passed away, but the beams of these humble buildings remain, and are now around you.

SOUTH CHEAM.

The district in Cheam lying to the south of the Thanet Sands had no houses on it (except the Warren) until the Water Company's mains came in 1864. After that a few houses were built, but in 1901 the only houses south of the railway were a few in Sandy Lane, viz., " Coldblow," " Stone Lodge," and " Mayfield," and three houses in Peach's Close. In 1901 two houses were built in Burdon Lane, and from them fields extended up to the Downs, and no more were built until about 1910. North of the railway the fields between the Cheam Road and the railway were laid out with roads and built upon about 1906.

About 1900 the old track that was the continuation of Gander Green Lane was laid out as a road and called York Road, and Cornwall Road was laid out at the same time; but no houses had been built upon them. Until about 1910 Mulgrave Road came to an end at Overton Road, but about that date the land on the east side of Burdon Lane was bought by the British Land Co., Mulgrave Road was continued on to Burdon Lane, Arundel and Beresford Roads were made, and the old track from Hale's Bridge to Burdon Lane was made into Manor Road. In 1928 the By-pass Road was made, so that through traffic going north and south avoided passing through Sutton, and the old Hale's Bridge was replaced with a new one to carry the By-pass.

Sir Edwin Landseer, R.A., the painter of animals, lived in a house that stood on the south side of the Cheam Road where Landseer Road is now.

Belmont is at the southern end of both Cheam and Sutton, where the parishes join the North Downs. This part was all fields until about 1865, and the only house on it was Sutton Farm, now called Sutton Lodge, and the South Metropolitan District School, which was built in 1852. The line from Sutton to Epsom Downs was made in 1865, and a station was put at this spot, which was called " California." An inn was built near the station about this time called the California Arms—so named, according to local tradition, because the land about there had been bought as a building speculation by a man who had made money during the Californian gold rush. Later on the name of the station was changed to " Belmont "—a name suggested, it is said, by the wife of the station-master. Unfortunately, the building speculation was badly planned, for the first thing that was done was to build a row of shops, though there were no houses near to provide any customers. For years this row of shops stood empty and desolate with fields round them, but about thirty years ago the land got into better hands, good and appropriate houses were built, and the errors of the start were forgotten. Situated as Belmont is, high up on the chalk at the edge of the Downs, it is an ideal position for a residential district.

CHEAM COMMON, which was really a common in bygone days, stretched from the north end of the parish at Worcester Park nearly half-way up Pond Hill. Not so very long ago the old gateway was still standing which was erected in 1790. The main London Road crossed the Common by the Queen Victoria Inn, at which spot the old toll gate used to stand. The Epsom–London Road crossed it from east to west and the Malden and Cheam Common Roads from south to north. At the extreme corner, about where the Huntsman Hall Inn now stands, there was once a cross called " Lynce's Corner," which marked where the three parishes of Cheam, Sutton and Malden met. It seems to have been at the side of an old road, " Green Lanes," running from Ewell eastwards towards Mitcham. The Huntsman's Hall stands at the corner where Green Lanes crosses Cheam Common Road. The inn is an old one, but the date at which it was established is unknown. The London to Epsom Road crossed the Common from east to west and intersected the Malden Road, and at this point on the Malden Road used to stand a turnpike, until it was removed about 1882. There is now an inn at this corner, the " Queen Victoria," probably established soon after Queen Victoria came to the throne.

Further east, along the Epsom–London Road, is another inn, the " Lord Nelson." There is a print of the Lord Nelson Inn in a series called *Scenes on the Road, or a trip to Epsom and back*, published in 1838, showing various types of cabriolets and chariots and a small cart drawn by two dogs. The building shown on this print is now incorporated in Saint Anthony's Hospital, and forms part of the nurses' quarters. The present Lord Nelson Inn is a little lower down the hill.

The first engagement between the Royalist and Parliamentary armies in 1643 took place in Worcester Park, in the avenue leading to Worcester House, which is in the parish of Malden. The Royalist army was defeated and retreated across this piece of Cuddington and Cheam Common, through Cheam in the direction of Putney. Probably the spur found in Parkside, Cheam (page 36), and the three soldiers buried in Cheam Churchyard (page 36), have to do with this battle.

Cheam may also have been disturbed by some other fighting which took place near Banstead and Ewell, during the rising in Surrey under the Duke of Buckingham in 1648. The fighting began at Banstead, and the Parliamentary troops retreated to Ewell and managed to ambush and defeat the Royalist troops at that place. Cheam must have felt the effects of fighting so near, but no records of it have been found in Cheam. The author has an ornamental bronze gilt spur found in Nork Park, Banstead, of about Charles I period, which may be a relic of the engagement. A description of this period may be found in a local novel about " Nonsuch," by Anne L. Glynn, called *A Pearl of the Realm*.

In 1933 the Parish of Cuddington was split up and divided between Ewell and the Borough of Sutton and Cheam, the amount allotted to Sutton and Cheam being 531 acres. The piece received by the Borough was in two portions, each being of an irregular triangular shape. The portion added to the south-eastern boundary of Cheam was probably part of the Nonsuch Little Park, and the part added to the north-eastern boundary part of the Nonsuch Great Park or Worcester Park.

The Cuddington Court Golf Course is on the south piece of Cuddington, and the Saxon burial (mentioned on page 10) was found while making one of the bunkers.

A large portion of the north triangular part was a large farm belonging to the house called Stoneleigh, which stood on the west side of the Cheam Common Road where the cinema now stands. This district has all been laid out for building, and a new station called " Stoneleigh " was opened by the Southern Railway in 1935.

This part of Worcester Park and Cuddington was all open fields until about 1865, when building was commenced at Longfellow Road.

POTTERY. In April, 1923, the author was sent for to see some pottery that had been dug up when a soak-away was being made behind a new house in Parkside called " Springfield," that was in course of erection. These proved to be a number of mediæval earthenware jugs that were lying thickly under the ground at this spot. Permission to dig further was given, and an enormous number of pots of various shapes, and great quantities of earthenware fragments, were discovered, all mixed up with wood ashes. At one part a floor formed of chalk and clay had been laid over these fragments, and on breaking through this floor the acrid smell of the wood ashes was very pungent, although these wood ashes must have been buried for some 600 years, as the floor was probably laid down in the thirteenth century. It would seem that there had been a pottery works

Excavation of Kiln.

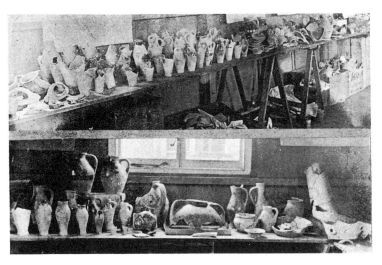

Some of the Pottery found.

there in the thirteenth century, and a kiln was finally unearthed. After the kiln had fallen out of use a shed was built near it, and the ground was levelled up with heaps of waste pottery

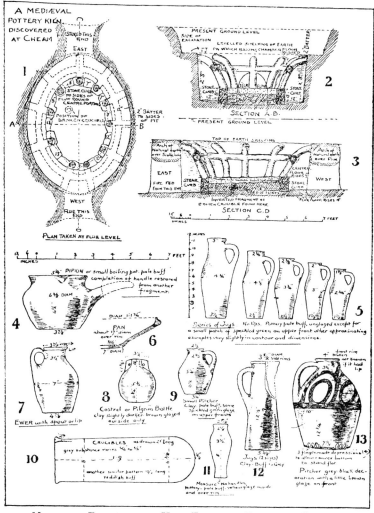

MEDIÆVAL POTTERY AND KILN FOUND IN PARKSIDE, CHEAM.

1. Plan of kiln.	6. Milk pan.	11. Measure.
2. Section A.B.	7. Ewer.	12. Jug.
3. Section C.D.	8. Pilgrim bottle.	13. Pitcher.
4. Cooking pot.	9. Small pitcher.	
5. Series of jugs.	10. Crucible.	

taken from the refuse heap where they had thrown all the waste bits of pottery, and this was covered with a layer of chalk and clay to make a floor for the shed. Of some hundreds of pots that were found, all were defective, which accounted for their being thrown away. The kiln itself was removed and is now set up in the Science Museum in South Kensington. The kiln was dug in the chalk as an oval on plan, about 5′ × 7′ and about 2′ 6″ deep. There was a slightly raised portion in the centre formed of flints, covered level with finely ground burnt clay. The chalk sides were covered with a layer of clay, and this was kept in position by flying buttresses made with clay plastered round a withey bent into position. There was probably also a central pillar, as rebuilt at the Science Museum, but this was not found. Over this was a flooring of tiles. The pottery to be burnt was arranged on this, and a clay covering (a sagger) was put all over it, shutting the pottery in. A fire was then lighted outside and the heat passed under the kiln to the flue at the other end. When the pottery was burnt, the covering sagger was broken up and the pots removed. Of the pottery found, about 120 pieces were good enough for museums and they have been distributed to the British Museum, the Victoria and Albert Museum at Kensington, the Guildford Museum, and to the collection in the Old Cottage at Cheam. The clay seems to have been dug from what is now the extension of the churchyard. It was very excellent ware, chiefly of jugs and dishes of various kinds. Some were partly glazed with a lead glaze. For instance, the only part of the jugs that was glazed was where the drip would come from the spout. Probably the lead ore (galena), which came from Derbyshire, was expensive. The Cheam potters appear to have carried their wares to London for sale, as there are specimens of the Cheam pottery, that have been found in excavations in London, in both the Guildhall and the London Museums. Some of the pitchers had foliated and geometrical patterns painted on them with a red oxide paint, and these are drawn very freely. As this pottery would have to be carried up to London on the backs of pack mules, there must have been a great deal of loss through breakages in transit. Two fairly complete crucibles were found, one of which is in the Old Cottage, which were made from a seam of white clay that is found in the extension of the churchyard, most of which is found to have been disturbed, no doubt for the purpose of getting this white clay. Milk pans were also made in large numbers, some of them eighteen inches or more in diameter. These had anti-splash rims, so that they could be moved without the milk splashing over. Leyland says:

> Crompton of London hath a close at Cuddington, in Southery (Surrey) where the King buildeth. In this close is a value of fine yerth to make moldes for goldsmiths and casters of metale, that a load of it sold for a crown of gold. Like yerth is not found in all England.

Camden's *Britannia* (edition 1610) says :

> About foure miles from the Thamis within the Country, Nonesuch, a retiring place of the Prince, putteth downe and surpasseth all other houses round about; which the most magnificent Prince King Henrie the Eighth, in a very healthful place called Cuddington before selected for his own delight and ease, and built with so great sumptiousnesse and rare workmanship, that it aspireth to the top of osten- tation for show————Neere hereunto (and worth the noting it is) there is a value of potters earth highly commended and therefore sold the deerer for the making of those crucibles and small vessels which goldsmiths use in melting their gold.

In the *History of Banstead* (written by Sir Henry Lambert) it is recorded that in 1374 John, potter of Cheyham (Cheam), sold for a shilling each two figures of knights on horseback to Banstead Manor House. These figures of knights on horse- back are very rare and valuable. No doubt John, the potter, made them in Cheam, and probably the kiln in which he made them, and his heap of spoilt specimens, are still lying under the soil of some Cheam garden, and the lucky owner of the garden may discover them at any time. There can be no doubt that there are many of these mediæval pottery kilns still to be un- covered in Cheam, and it is to be hoped that the finders will appreciate the value of their discovery and not simply destroy them. A full description of the kiln and the pottery is given in *Surrey Archæological Collections*, vol. xxxv.

This summer (1936) the site of another pottery kiln has been discovered at 19, High Street, Cheam. An addition to the back of the house was being made, when a quantity of pots, in good condition, were found; but unfortunately the workmen did not realise the importance of the discovery, so they broke them up and threw them back under the foundations. Only a few pieces were recovered, but these proved that this pottery was exactly similar to that made at the Parkside kiln discovered in 1923. Some digging has been done near where these pots were found and quantities of wood ashes, mixed with fragments of this thirteenth-century pottery, and lumps of clay suitable for making pottery, were uncovered. This seems to prove that another kiln must have stood on this spot in the thirteenth century. Among the fragments found were portions of handles, some of which had been secured to the pot with " skewer " or " dowel " joints; but some had no means of securing them to the pot and they had broken away. In the 1923 kiln no handles were found that did not have some sort of dowelling to fasten them to the pot. In the sixteenth century the existing house was built over the site of the kiln.

CHEAM POOR RATES, 1730 to 1753. An old resident allowed these extracts to be made from the old rate book of Cheam, which was in his possession, and they show some of the quaint items of parish expenditure in those days. The spelling and capitals, or absence of them, are as in the original:

Oct. ye 19	Paid fr old Stokers Cofin		7	0
	paid ye parson and clark for Beiring old Stoker		3	0
	paid Goode fillins for nursing old Stoker		1	6
Mar 19 1736	Payd ye clark for ringen ye bell		2	0
Jan 11 1741	For a shroud for Bridgetts child			7
Aug 1 1741	Paid the Parson and clark for burying the womans child that had ye smallpox		3	0
Sept 7	Paid fr making 6 shifts for Dancer children		2	0
Oct 4	Paid Stephen Bundell for a fort-night nursing Bridgett Pullen in ye smallpox	£2	0	0
Oct 4 1742	paid fr a hankeshef fr Edward Goldsmith		1	0
Oct 26	paid fr a nack of mutton fr Jo. Phipps		1	2
Dec 5	paid Dame Badger fr fiering		4	0
Jan 1742/43	paid fr a poor woman Loging			2

Ap	4		paid Dame Bully fr shirt buttons fr franklin children		4
June	23	1745	fr washing Danoll Franckling 4 shirts	1	6
Jan	24	1746	paid fr shift and throd fr Mary James	3	6
Ap	4		charge fr going to Darcken [Dorking ?]	5	0
Ap	5		paid John Hockons for menden the Tillin of the Alms hous	2	10½
Feb	2	1747	Paid Bryants wife for mending Ed Gouldsmith	6	0
May	31		Paid for Shop goods for a poor man that fel Ill	4	1
			Paid to A poor Wooman in distress	1	0
Ap	24	1748	Paid for Phisick for Jupp girl	1	0
Oct	23		Paid Scrivans ye Taylor fr making James Franklyn a wastecoat and Britches out of ye old	2	3
Sep	23	1753	To a woman and 4 children very noisey	1	0
Dec	27		Dorin had a pair of Butes		

It will be interesting to ratepayers to know what the rates of Cheam used to be.

In 1732 the rate for the first half of the year was 3d. in the £, which produced £13 0s. 6d., and for the second half it was 2d. in the £, producing £8 11s. 9d. On this year the rate paid by the Duke of Bedford for West Cheam Manor was 15s., and the Parsonage paid £2 13s. 4d.

In 1746 the rates had risen considerably, as the first rate produced £17 18s. 4d., and the second rate £35 16s. 8d.

The average of the Poor Rates for the years 1783, 1784, and 1785, according to Manning and Bray, was:

	CHEAM			SUTTON		
Average amount collected ..	£166	16	1	£183	17	2
Average expended on County purposes, such as vagrants, militia, bridges, etc. ..	29	14	10	19	11	10
Average for the poor	137	1	3	164	5	4

Deduct for expenses, Law, Attendance on Justice, Removals, Parish Meetings, etc.

Cheyham: £14 4s. 2d. Sutton: £18 14s. 5d.

but it is not stated what these expenses are to be deducted from.

This method of raising money for the support of the poor was first levied in the reign of Elizabeth, and later on certain social services were added, in the case of Cheam and Sutton for the militia and bridges. In Elizabeth's time it was intended to be an income tax, not a tax on people's standard of living. There was no exact method of arriving at people's income, so it was assumed that everyone spent one tenth of their income on the rent of their house; therefore if the rent of the house was taxed it would come to the same thing as taxing their income. It was an excellent idea if the theory that people spent a tenth of their income on rent was correct, but as things are now it is incorrect. People do not necessarily spend one tenth of their income on rent, but still this quaint old custom of raising money for all social services by a tax on the size of the house still continues. If you are rich you may perhaps spend only a small portion of your income on rent, as a small house may suit your purpose better; but if you are poor, and have a large family, you have to spend much more than the tenth. To give two actual examples:

One is of a lady with at least £2,000 a year, who lives in a house of £30 rental, with rates £12 10s. 0d., equal to 1½d. in the £ on her income.

The other is of a man with a large family getting £2 a week. He has to take a house at 7/6 a week and the rates come to 2/6, so that he is paying at the rate of 1/3 in the £ on his income.

Moreover, if his family increases the house may become over-crowded, in which case the authorities, quite rightly, make him take a larger house, when not only will he have to pay more rent, but he will have to pay more rates, though his income would remain the same.

The rates in Elizabeth's time were only for the support of the poor (except in special cases, such as Cheam and Sutton, where some went for upkeep of bridges and militia), but last century more public services were added, which did not exist in the time of Elizabeth, such as Police, Street Lighting, Drainage, Fire-protection, Education, Roads, etc., and last of all, Housing.

It is a quaint old survival from Tudor times, but now that there is a complete machinery for ascertaining people's incomes it seems rather a primitive way of raising money by taxing their standard of living. No doubt it will be realised some day what a stupid anachronism this method of raising money really is, and a better and more up-to-date scheme will be worked out; and in a few years people will look back on the present rating system with the same contempt and amusement with which we look at the old window tax of the Georgian period.

CHEAM FAIR. The origin of Cheam Fair, which is still held in Park Road on the 15th of May in every year, dates back for many centuries.

It is believed that in 1259 Henry III granted leave for a weekly market on Tuesdays and an annual fair on May 15th and 16th, to be held in the village of Kaham. The weekly market has long since died out, but the annual fair has survived to the present day, except that after 1680 it ceased to be a two-day affair and is now only held on May 15th.

This old site is no doubt the same one where the fair has been held since 1259. The author has an old deed for the sale of some land in Cheam in which one of the boundaries is given as " The Market Furlong." This piece of Park Lane where the fair is held is just a furlong in length. The old boundary wall of West Cheam Manor stood where the front garden fences of the houses now stand, and the fair occupies exactly this piece of ground in front of the fences. Malden Road has been widened, so that Park Lane is now a little shorter than it formerly was. However, the showmen put their booths right out into the Malden Road, as far as Park Lane originally extended. Now that houses have been built in Park Lane it makes no difference, and the booths, swings and cocoanut shies still occupy the whole of the lane right up to the garden railings.

There are only two ways in which the Fair could be stopped —by Act of Parliament, or if no one turned up on the eventful day to peg out their pitch. It is, however, a most inconvenient spot to hold a fair, and must be a great inconvenience to the residents in Park Road. It would be a great pity to entirely abolish an old custom such as this Fair, which has been in existence for over 650 years, and perhaps the authorities may be able to arrive at some arrangement for holding it in some more convenient spot.

During the war the Fair dwindled considerably, but it has never been allowed to cease.

The gipsies and their caravans arrive usually the night before and depart early on the morning of the following day. They are very decent people and give no trouble.

CHEAM WAR MEMORIAL. The war memorial was erected by the subscriptions of the people in Cheam, and was erected from designs by the author in part of the garden of West Cheam Manor, which was presented to the village by Mrs. Bethell of Cheam Park. The walls surrounding the memorial are part of the original walls of the Manor, lowered from their original height of twelve feet. The design is a cross on a column, and the whole scheme, with its decoration, is emblematic of sacrifice. As an essential part of the design, stone seats were placed on each side of the memorial, and these, with the gun which was originally placed at the east side, and the line of the steps at the front, broadened the base, and greatly added to the balance and dignity of the design. The gun was an integral part of the design, to emphasise the horrors of war. A gun with a strong horizontal line was selected, with harsh, strong, brutal lines, in violent contrast to the memorial, where every line was softened and there is not a straight line in it. Many lines may appear to be straight, but they all curve somewhat to soften the general effect. A few years ago the gun was removed, for some reason that the author has never been able to discover, and nothing was put in its place, those removing the gun evidently not realising how necessary it really was to have a strong horizontal line at this point. It might have been thought that those who went to the expense of removing the gun would have put a stone seat in its place so as not to upset the balance of the design, but nothing has ever been done. The carving and erecting of the memorial were excellently carried out by a local mason, Mr. Snook of Worcester Park.

A War Memorial Chapel was also erected in the church, where the names of the fallen are again repeated on two plaques on the walls. Among the names is that of Flight-Commander F. Brock, who invented the smoke screen, and who was killed at Zeebrugge.

War Memorial, Cheam.

During the war many Belgian refugees were given hospitality, first from October, 1914, at Coldblow, and after February, 1916, at the White House, and altogether about fifty refugees passed through the home.

A very active detachment of V.A.D.'s was formed during the war which did a great deal of good work, the members serving in different hospitals in England; one serving in France for several years, and another nursing in Salonica. The detachment (Surrey 136) is still very active and is doing good work under its commandant, Mrs. Owens, and has its own permanent headquarters in the Malden Road.

CHEAM CHARITIES.   Cheam is particularly rich in Parish Charities. Some of them coming from old bequests are centuries old. Foremost among them in Smith's Charity. Henry Smith, who left a legacy to Cheam, died in 1628. He appears to have been a man of somewhat unusual character. He seems to have been exceedingly wealthy, and at one time was a City Alderman. His hobby was walking through every village in Surrey and Sussex, dressed in tattered clothing and pretending to be a beggar. He always took his dog with him, which earned him the nickname of " Dog Smith." To those villages who treated him well he left a legacy to be used for the poor. It is pleasant to think that Cheam was one of these, for the village received £4 10s. a year from a farm in Sussex.

Altogether the eccentric Mr. Smith left forty-nine legacies to parishes in Surrey. Only three parishes in this county were omitted, and one of these, it is said, received a whip instead of a legacy, which seems to suggest that there was something wrong with the inhabitants' manners. He is buried at Wandsworth, and a monument is erected there to his memory.

There is also the Peirson Charity. Samuel Peirson, of Cheam, who died August 27th, 1699, and his wife Anne, died 25th October, 1728, left to the Cheam poor "a cottage, a barn, and three acres of land for relief of the poor, to be vested in the Minister for the time being and the possessor of the house occupied by Mr. Kimpson." This house was the White House.

A legacy for the poor was also left by George Aldrich, of Whitehall, Headmaster of Cheam School, who died in 1685.

In 1824 Sir Edmund Antrobus, of Lower Cheam House, gave £1,000 to keep his family tomb in order and the surplus to go to the poor.

There is also a Lumley Chapel Trust, dated 1864, in which a sum of money was to be used for repairs to the chapel and the surplus to be invested until stock exceeded £100 for the poor of the parish, subject to such repairs.

In 1872 Mr. J. T. Martin gave £107 for poor relief.

For the year 1924 these Charities amounted to £121, which is now distributed by the Consolidated Charities under the Charity Commissioners.

SUTTON.

The Parish of Sutton lies on the east side of Cheam, and is nearly of the same size. Cheam had an area of 1,909 acres and Sutton had 1836. Like Cheam, the first settlement was on the Thanet Sands, which in the High Street extend from St. Nicholas' Road to Angel Hill, and this was the only part where good water could be obtained. On this part the church, manor-house and village were founded.

Like Cheam, the Manor of Sutton, or Sutton Abbas, or Sudtone, was included in the alleged gift to Chertsey Abbey in 727, and certainly in 1066 the Abbey of St. Peter, Chertsey, held land in Sutton which was assessed at ten hides in the time of King Edward, and later at 8½ hides. In the Saxon charters a wood of the name of Thundersfield is mentioned as being in connection with Sutton, but it is not known where this was. It may have been in quite another district, as it was not unusual for a parish to have another part in quite a different place. Domesday mentions two churches in Sutton, which were worth £20 before the Conquest, and £15 in 1086. There is no trace of a second church in Sutton, and it has been suggested that this second church may have been at Thundersfield. The name Thundersfield suggests a connection with Thor, the god of Thunder.

Domesday Book says that the Abbot of Chertsey holds Sudtone.

In the time of King Edward it was assessed at 30 hides; now at 8½ hides. There are 2 carucates in the demesne, and 29 villains and 4 cottars with 13 carucates There are 2 churches, and 2 bondmen, and 2 acres of meadow. The wood yields 10 swine. In the time of King Edward it was valued at 20 pounds, now at 15 pounds.

A "plough-land" or "carucate" was as much land as a man could till in a year with one plough and team. "Villains" were labourers who had a certain portion of land allotted to them, for which they were dependent on their lord, and bound to do certain work and corporeal service. "Cottars" were a class of slightly superior privileges. A "hide" was a piece of land from 60 to 100 acres.

This would seem to show that there would be about 200 inhabitants in Sutton at that time, and that there would be about thirty houses.

In 1538 Henry VIII purchased the Manor of Sutton, together with those of Ebisham (Epsom), Coulsdon, and Horley, from the Abbot of Chertsey, and in the same year granted them to Sir Nicholas Carew of Beddington. On the attainder of Sir Nicholas for treason, the King seized these Manors, and they remained in the hands of the Crown till Edward VI granted part of them to Thomas, Lord D'Arcy of Cliche, but kept the Manors of Sutton, Ebisham and Coulsdon in his own hands. When Queen Mary came to the throne she restored the whole of these Manors to Francis, only son of Sir Nicholas Carew.

John Evelyn records that in October, 1632, he visited Lady D'Arcy at Sutton. Lady D'Arcy's son married Evelyn's sister.

At a later date the Manor again came into the hands of the Crown, but the reason for this is not known. However, in 1663 Charles II granted it to the Duke of Portland. In 1669 the Duke of Portland sold the Manor to Sir Robert Long, who, in the same year, sold it again to Sir Richard Mason. Sir Richard Mason's daughter, Dorothy, married Sir William Brownlow. She died in 1700, and there is a monument to her in St. Nicholas' Church, now concealed by the organ.

In 1716 the Manor was again sold, and was bought by Henry Cliffe, an East India Captain, and it remained in the Cliffe family till it was bought by Hertford College, Oxford, in 1831. The advowson of the church has always been in the hands of the Lords of the Manor, and is now in the gift of Hertford College, Oxford.

There was a smaller Manor in the parish, which was held in the reign of King John by Gilbert Bassett, and in the reign of Edward III (in 1372) by Simon de Codyngton, but nothing more is known about it.

Pope Alexander granted a bull conferring to the Abbey of Chertsey a moiety of the tithes of Sutton, but it does not appear that the appropriation was ever carried into effect. The living, however, paid a pension to the Abbey of 13s. 4d. It was a Rectory in the Deanery of Ewell. In 1259 it was valued at twenty marks, and it stands in the *Liber Regis* at £16 8s. 4d., paying 8s. 5d. for procurations and synodals.

At one time there appear to have been vineyards in Sutton, as in many other places, as in a roll of the debts of the Prior and Convent of Merton, in the early part of the reign of Henry II (1154–1189), there appears the item: That they had borrowed forty marks upon the security of their vineyard in Sudtone (Sutton), Surrey.

These are the boundaries of the parish of Sutton as given at the time of Thomas Pigot, Abbot of Chertsey, in the reign of Henry VII, 1496:

> They begin at the Inclosure of Robert de Cheyham, go to the Hale on the North, thence to Innemere, and thence to Pliisford Bridge, thence to Wollardsfelde on the East, go up to Hetchecroft on the South, thence to the South side of Kynwardesley Field, thence descend in the two eldeseldes to Kedeston, thence South by the East side of Fernhill to Greenhill, thence South to Drolkenests and thence to Esthalds, thence to Cayneres Bushe, and thence to Betheman, and thence down to Dolleway to Alveslaweshull, and so down by the Byshopp's———to Hertesden on the West, thence North West to Beteburewe, thence to the Inhome of Robert de Cheyham above mentioned.

On one of the Rogation days, that is on the Monday, Tuesday, or Wednesday before Ascension Day, the parish boundaries used to be beaten, when a procession of the parish officers and parishioners used to walk all round the boundaries to see if they had been infringed in any way. This was done in Sutton in 1867, but had not been done for sixty years before.

The name Benhilton appears at various times as " Bon Hill," " Been Hill," and " Benhill."

The Abbot of Chertsey granted to the Lords of the Manor of Sutton-Abbot the right to erect a gallows, a pillory and a cucking-stool. A cucking-stool was a machine used for the punishment of scolds and brawling women, also a punishment inflicted on brewers and bakers who transgressed the laws. It was a chair fixed on the end of a long pole, which was hinged on a wooden frame. The pole, with the victim securely fastened into the chair at the end of it, was pushed out over a pond, and then they were ducked as many times as the sentence prescribed.

It is not known if these privileges were ever used, but there certainly was an execution in 1768. The *St. James' Chronicle* (a paper published three times a week, price $2\frac{1}{2}d$.) for the issue

Tuesday, April 19th, to Thursday, April 21st, 1768, has the following notice:

> Monday, at the execution of William Palmer, for Forgery, with Anderson and Stevenson for Housebreaking, upon Sutton Common near that town, a Hearse appearing with Coffins for the two last named Malefactors under Pretence that they were sent by their friends from Croydon, the Fallacy was detected and proved to be a scheme of two Surgeons to have the bodies for Dissection, wherepon the Populace put the Corpses into the Coffins, each with all the clothes and Halters about their Necks, and so carried and buried them in Kingston Church Yard with their Brother Sufferer, the Funeral Service being performed by the Curate. The Populace whilst this was doing, cut the traces of the Horses belonging to the Hearse and damaged the same, then fell upon the Surgeons and their Mob, cut the Horsemen's bridles and by pelting them with Pebble stones they were obliged to quit the Field in great Disorder, sorely cut and Mangled. The Executioner who felt the Resentment of the Populace for following the Bodies to the Church Yard and claiming their Clothing as his Perquisite, without which he and his Companions were obliged to decamp.

The present main roads in Sutton are of comparatively recent construction, and it is difficult to trace the course of the old original roads. The Brighton Road was the first main road coming near Sutton, and this was constructed in 1755, and brought Sutton into contact with the outside world, as it formed the main road from London to Brighton till 1809, when the road through Croydon was made.

The original road in Sutton, running east to west, was not the present Cheam Road, but one that can be traced running from the High Street along West Street, Camden Road, Tate Road, through Love Lane, to Cheam. The present Cheam and Carshalton Roads were not constructed till 1755, before which time they must only have been tracks over the common fields.

The present Sutton High Street was probably a narrow road with the wall of the Manor House on the east side—a high red brick wall, which was not pulled down till about 1900. The High Street probably continued as a track southwards to Banstead and Woodmansterne, and northwards to Merton, where it would join the London–Epsom Road.

Before the road from London entered Sutton there was a

St. Nicholas' Church in 1806.

The "Plough," Sutton Common Road, 1912 (*see* p. 98).

steep little bit of hill beside Benhilton, known as Angel Hill from the name of an inn standing there; but a cutting was made through this about 1810–1820. It is said that this cutting was made by order of the Regent, who used the Brighton Road very frequently on his many journeys to Brighton, as it was a nasty little bit of hill at the end of the first stage, when the horses were tired, for fresh horses were put in when the coach arrived at the Cock. It is also said that the reason why George IV used the Sutton-Brighton Road instead of the Croydon one was because it made the distance from London to Brighton just under fifty miles, while the road through Croydon was over fifty miles, and some special council had to be appointed if the King was more than fifty miles away from London.

It is recorded in Machyn's Diary that on May 25th, 1553, an earthquake occurred in Sutton and the surrounding districts, but it was not a very severe one as the diary says " pottes, panes, and dysys dounst, and most felle downe about house and with many odur thyngs."

In 1841 the only dissenting place of worship was a small chapel for Independent Methodists.

Now, in 1936, besides the Parish Church of St. Nicholas, there are: All Saints', Benhilton, erected in 1866; St. Barnabas in 1884, and Christ Church in 1888. Also there is a church belonging to the Roman Catholics, " Our Lady of the Rosary," built in 1892; to the Baptists, in the Cheam Road, opened in 1935 (replacing one that stood in the High Street that was opened in 1883); to the Methodists in the Cheam, Lind and Marshall's Roads ; one at Belmont to the Congregationalists in Carshalton Road and Benhill Street; and others belonging to the New Baptists, Christian Scientists, Spiritualists, and the Salvation Army.

In 1841 the number of children being educated in the Parish Schools was 170. Now (1936) there are 3,222 children in the elementary schools in Sutton, and 2,256 in those of Cheam.

ST. NICHOLAS' CHURCH. A church appears to have stood on the site of the present church from Saxon times, which was altered and enlarged from time to time, and was held by the Abbey of Chertsey, one of these alterations being made at the end of the thirteenth century by the Abbot, John de Rutherwyk.

There are no remains of this old building, as the church was pulled down in 1864 and rebuilt on the same site, from the designs of Edwin Nash.

The old church is thus described by Manning and Bray in 1808: " The Church consists of a Nave and Chancel only. In length it is 23 yards and in breadth 12½ yards. The Chancel is raised 3 steps above the Nave. There is no stained glass. The font is modern. The tower at the West end was of wood, but was rebuilt with brick a few years ago. There are the remains of some characteristic inscriptions on the outside of one of the North windows."

Aubrey, writing in the middle of the seventeenth century, says that outside the north window was a Latin inscription cut in the stone—" PRI – PUR – WILLEM – SOUL – ALICIE – MAT – ILLIS "—which he renders " Pray for William Soul and Alice His Mother."

The altar of the old church was on the place where the altar of the Lady Chapel of the present church now stands. The eighteenth-century memorial slab inscribed with the name of " Robert Holmes, Esq," now lying on the floor of the south aisle, just below the Lady Chapel altar steps, was once in the nave of the old church.

Manning and Bray describe the following monuments, which were in the old church:

> On the South wall of the Chancel on a pyramid of black marble are the Arms of Earl Talbot in white marble, with the motto *Humani nihil aliemum*. At the top is an elegant white urn depressed; below in white marble two censers burning in saltire across a crown of laurel. Below: "To the memory of William Earl Talbot Baron of Hensol. He was created Earl Talbot in 1761, and Baron Dynevor in 1780. In 1761 he was created Lord Steward of His Majesty's Household. His Lordship married Mary, daughter of, and heiress of, Adam Cardonnel Esq., by whom he had two children. A daughter alone survived him. He died April 27th 1782, aged 72 years, and is interred in a vault near this place with his mother Cecil, daughter and heiress to Charles Matthews Esq., of Castlemerryck, Glamorganshire."

> On the North wall of the Chancel is a beautiful marble monument, railed in, with the arms of Brownlowe, and the inscription: " Here lies the body of Dame Dorothy Brownlowe, wife of Sir William Brownlowe, of Belton, in the

OLD SUTTON.

The "Cock," 1899.

The "Greyhound," 1893.

Back view of the "Cock," 1899.

The "Cricketers" in 1908.

County of Lincoln, Bart., eldest daughter and co-heiress of Sir Richard Mason, Knight and Controller of the Green Cloath to King Charles, and King James II and of Dame Ann his wife, who departed this life on the 13th January 1699–1700 in the 34th year of her age."

These monuments are refixed in the present church, but the one to Lady Brownlowe is entirely concealed by the organ. It appears to have been a rich, but not very beautiful piece of sculpture, if one may judge by the description that was given of it by Hone, who visited Sutton in 1831, and thus described it: " She is represented in a recumbent position with three sorrowing infants about her, and four cherubs above, in a sort of dish of hasty pudding, garnished with slices of gilt ginger-bread."

On the north wall of the old church was a black marble monument to Mrs. Sarah Glover, late wife of Mr. Joseph Glover, rector of Sutton (1630), with the verses:

> This monument present unto your view,
> A woman rare, in whom all grace divine,
> Faith, love, zeale, piety, in splendid hue,
> With sacred knowledge perfectly did shine.
> Since then examples teach, learne you by this,
> To mount the stepps of everlasting bliss.

On the north wall of the chancel of the old church was a small white marble monument to Isaac Littlebury, traveller and linguist, who died 30th April, 1710, aged 53 years. This is refixed in the present church at the west end of the south aisle.

Isaac Littlebury was the son of a bookseller living in Covent Garden. He could speak many languages and was chiefly known for his translations of Herodotus.

In the chancel of the church, supported by a bracket, is a helmet, but the history of it is unknown. Probably it was a funeral helmet and was placed there at the funeral of Earl Talbot, who died in 1782.

Aubrey (middle of seventeenth century) describes a mutilated brass that was before the altar which read:

> .... lyeth sumtyme of thys
> .... day of Apryll yn the yere
> .... os soule Jhu have mercy. Amen.

But this had entirely disappeared in 1808. Another brass that was near the altar and described by Aubrey, but which had also disappeared in 1808, was inscribed: " Pray for the soule of Sir John Wyrley, late parson of Cheyham. All chrysen soulles of your charite say a pater moster Ao 1557."

In the churchyard, near the east end of the church, there is a tombstone with this inscription:

> Here resteth in peace, the body of William Juniper Esq. who departed this life Dec. 11 1812. Aged 56 years. Late Smith of Southwark, and to the honourable Board of Ordnance; and of Juniper Hall, in this Parish.
> My Sledge and Hammer lie declined,
> My Bellows, too, have lost their wind;
> My Fire's extinct, my forge decayed,
> And in the dust my Vice is laid.
> My Coals are spent, my Iron's gone,
> My Nails are drove, my Work is done.
> My Fire-dried Corpse lies here at rest;
> My Soul, Smoke-like, soars to be blest.

There is a record in the register of marriages at Carshalton that "Nathaneal Winter, Clerke, the Curate of Sutton was married unto Katherine Wroe, widow, the 14 December 1601."

In 1547 a valuation was made of the chantries held by the churches which were then seized by the Crown. Those in Sutton are described:

> Lampelightes used and mayneteyned within the Parysshe churche of Suttonne with yerely revenues gyven to that use for ever whiche are worth .... in landes by yere vj*d*.

Among the benefactions that have been given to the parish are:

1613   Henry Smith by will £1 19s. 0d. annually for the poor.

1774   Elizabeth Stephens by will £6 annually to be distributed among poor widows and housekeepers.

1782   Elizabeth Stephens £200 stock for cleaning and beautifying the church and chancel, and making good the footpaths of the parish.

1789   Mr. William Beed £200 South Sea Stock, the interest of which to be applied to the education of the poor of the parish, at the discretion of the Rector and Churchwardens.

1793   Mrs. Mary Gibson by will £500 3% consolidated Bank Annuities to be applied as follows: £5 to the Minister of Sutton for the time being for ever, for the preaching of a sermon on the 12th of August in every year; £5 to be distributed that day at Church among the poor; £1 to the clerk of the parish on that day; £4 to be divided among the Churchwardens on that day, on condition of their attending to the monument and family vault of the Gibsons, and seeing that it is kept in repair by the Governors and Guardians of Christ's Hospital. (This vault is still opened and inspected on Aug. 12th every year.)

1823 Mrs. Bentley left two sums of £50 each producing £4 6s. 2d. annually towards the support of the parish schools.

1829 Mrs. Lucy Manners the annual interest of £700 3% Consols. to be applied towards the education of the children of the poor at the discretion of the Rector.

LIST OF THE RECTORS OF ST. NICHOLAS', SUTTON.

Patrons	Incumbents	Institutions
Abbot and Convent o! Chertsey	Nicholas of Heddeshore	23 Oct. 1291
Do.	.. Richard de Barton ..	26 Sep. 1301
	(Register 1345–1366 lost)	
Do.	.. Roger de Mohante ..	was Rector 1362
Do.	.. John Peyntour de Ludgershall	12 Mar. 1377–8
Do.	.. John de Vyne ..	30 Jan. 1391–2
Do.	.. John Pynnere ..	18 May 1392
Do.	.. William Ferye ..	15 Oct. 1397
Do.	.. Robert Peek	30 Jan. 1397–8
Do.	.. William Greenefeld ..	16 Feb. 1401–2
Do.	.. John Baker was Rector	6 June 1411 and 17 Dec. 1412
	(Register 1415–1446 lost)	
Archb. of Canterbury on demise of the Abbot, dated 10 March 1448–9 pro hac vice	William Sotty ..	19 April 1451
The King for this turn	William Morland ..	13 Mar. 1461–2
King Henry VII ..	William Kelet ..	15 Nov. 1488
	(Register 1492–1500 lost)	
	George Grygge, LL.D.	died 1527
	William Benet, LL.D.	19 Mar. 1527–8
	—— Whight	was Rector 1534
	Richard Sedgrave ..	resigned 1539
The King	Richard Eliot ..	10 Feb. 1539–40
Do.	Miles Braithwaite, M.A.	17 July 1543

Queen Mary ..	Edmund Marvyn ..	4 July 1554
Henry Hungate, Citizen of London, for this and next turn	Thomas Halliday ..	8 Sept. 1568
Thomas Browker of Stoke; Thomas Chaplin of Mere, Wilts. In grant of Francis Carew for this turn	James Griffith ..	3 Mar. 1568-9
Sir Francis Carew ..	Ambrose Brigges ..	29 Dec. 1600
	Robert Cordell, M.A.	22 Mar. 1602-3
	(Register 1616–1628 lost)	
Edward Darcy of Dartford	Joseph Glover ..	resigned 1636
	Henry Wyche, M.A.	8 June 1636
Sir Richard Mason ..	George Roberts, M.A.	23 Sept. 1678
Richard Mason, Esq., *hac vice*	Jeremiah Oakley ..	4 Mar. 1685
Lady Ann Mason ..	William Stephens ..	26 July 1690
Thomas Case & Mary Blackman, *hac vice*	James Ramsey ..	10 Mar. 1717-18
Henry Cliff, Esq. ..	James Sanxay ..	31 Dec. 1745
Margaret Eleanor Cliffe, by advice of Susannah Cliffe, widow, her guardian ..	Giles Hatch	8 Jan. 1767
	Charles Gardener, D.D.	11 Mar. 1800
Hertford College, Oxford	Henry Hatch ..	9 May 1831
Do. ..	John Allen Giles, D.D.	1867
Do. ..	Chas. Thos. Crutwell, M.A.	17 Jan. 1885
Do. ..	Herbert Wm. Turner, M.A.	7 Feb. 1886
Do. ..	Edward Percy Woollcombe, O.B.E., M.A.	8 Sept. 1922

William Stephens, who was rector from 1690 to 1717, was well known, both for his writings and for his outspoken sermons. In 1694 he preached two sermons that were not considered flattering to King Charles the Martyr, one of these sermons being before the Lord Mayor at St. Mary-le-Bow. In 1700 he preached before members of the House of Commons at St. Margaret's, Westminster, and is said to have omitted the prayers for the Royal Family. This was considered an insult to the House, and led to a resolution being passed " that no person be recom-

OLD SUTTON.

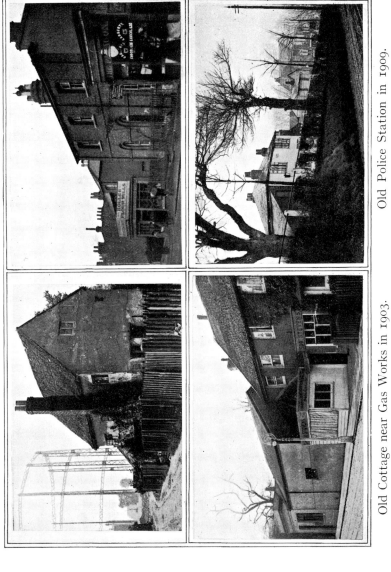

Old Cottage near Gas Works in 1903.
Stevens' Boot Shop in 1906.

Old Police Station in 1909.
Angel Hill in 1908.

mended to preach before this House in future who is under the dignity of a Dean in the Church, or hath not taken the degree of D.D." In 1707 Stephens published a letter reflecting on the Duke of Marlborough and Robert Harley, a Secretary of State for the Government. For this he was indicted before the Courts, was heavily fined, ordered to find sureties for his good behaviour for twelve months, and sentenced to stand in the pillory. The pillory was remitted, but not until he had been taken to Charing Cross and shown the preparations for carrying out the sentence.

James Sanxay, rector from 1745 till 1767, was the son of Dr. Sanxay who built Cheam School. He is buried in the churchyard.

John Allen Giles was rector from 1867 to 1884. He was born in 1808 and wished to become a barrister, but his mother persuaded him to enter the Church. He became headmaster of the City of London School, but resigned from it to become curate of Bampton, Oxfordshire. While there he wrote a book on the authenticity of the Books of the New Testament, called *Christian Records*, which caused much displeasure in the Church, and the Bishop of Oxford (Samuel Wilberforce) ordered the book to be suppressed. In 1855 he was tried at Oxford Assizes for having entered in the marriage register at Bampton Parish Church a marriage as having taken place on October 3rd which actually took place on the 5th, having himself performed the marriage out of canonical hours, soon after 6 p.m., having falsely entered that it was by license, and having forged the mark of a witness. He pleaded not guilty, as he had committed the offence out of good nature on behalf of one of his servants. He was sentenced to a year's imprisonment at Oxford Castle, but after three months he was released by Royal Warrant. Much sympathy was aroused by his imprisonment. After some time he was appointed rector of Sutton and remained there till his death in 1884.

About 1788 some of the London churches had collections to help poor churches in country districts, and on August 8th, 1788, a collection was taken at the church of St. Martin, Ludgate, towards the building of a steeple at Sutton church, for which £600 was required. The collection amounted to 9s. 7d. The steeple, no doubt, was the brick tower which replaced the old wooden one.

The following is an inventory of Church Ornaments belonging to St. Nicholas', Sutton, in 1552:

The inventory indentyd of all the goodes belles and ornamentes perteyning to the churche of Sutton in the Countye of Surrey made the 13th day of dessember in the vjth yere of the reign of our sovereign Lord Kyng Edward vjth by Thomas Rogers and John Smyth sydemen there sworn to present the same as hereafter followyth:

Imprimis iij belles. A lyttle belle callyd the sanctus bell. ij chalyses whereof one of them is all gylted. A coope of blewe velvyt. ij syrplyses. A vestement of whyte satin. A olde vestement. ij corporose cases wyth corporoces. ij grett candelstyckes of latten. ij lyttell candelstyckes of latten. ij aulter clothes of lynen. xij elles of lynen cloth for hosclyng towelles. A crosse of latten. A byble with the boke of servys. A paraphrase of Erasmus. A salter boke. ij albes.

These parcelles underwrytten were sold sense the first yere of the reign of our seyd sovereign Lord the Kyng as hereafter Folowyth.

Imprimis a Crosse of latten. vij li of wax. x bosses of latten for candelstyckes.

All these parcelles were sold by Geffrey Jowdrye and John Parker then churche wardens and by the consent of the hoole parishe the iiij yere of the reign of our seyd sovereign Lord the Kynges reign to Thomas Tasted of London for the summe of xiijs. iijd.

A crosse cloth of sylke which cloth with certen old banner clothes were sold to Myles Brafote (or Braithwaite) Parson of Sutton about the month of Februarye last past the seyd churche wardens and by lyke consent for the sume of xijs. all whiche seyd somes were employed by the consent of the hoole parishe about tylyng of the seyd churche and in byeng of lynen cloth and to other raparacions and necessaries about the seyd churche of Sutton.

Md. That Geffrey Jowdrye and Hughe Dyker were churche wardens in the first yere of the reign of our seyd sovereign Lord the Kynge.

Thomas Rogers } Sidesmen.
John Smithe

John Porter } Churchwardens.
Roger Lane

Saint Nicholas, Sutton.

Wardens: John Parker, Roger Lane.

OLD SUTTON.

St. Nicholas' Road in 1907.
St. Nicholas' Road in 1907.

High Street, near "Cricketers," in 1908.
The Green Pond in 1893.

Deliverid unto the wardens ther the xxvj day of May anno regnis Edwardi Sexto septimo by Sir Thomas Carwarden, Sir Thomas Saunder knightes John Scott Nicholas Leigh and William Saunder esquiors commissioners of our sovereign lorde the kynge among others within the countey of Surrey apointid for the sale of churche goodes these parcelles hereafter ensuing.

A chalice poz. xv oz. ij vestementes for the communion table.

Also remaining in their charge to the Kynges use iij belles in the steple and a sauns bell.

Received a chalice poz. xvj oz.

Sales.

Brasse and latten poz. xxxvij*lb*. vj*s*. ij*d*. One cope blew velvet sold for iiij*li*. xij*d*. Summa iiij*li*. vij*s*. ij*d*.

The Myles Brafote, parson, referred to the rector, Miles Braithwaite, who it is said was deprived of his living for marriage.

It will be seen that the money realised from the sale of certain of these church ornaments was devoted to the repair of the church, with the consent of the whole parish.

SUTTON REGISTERS. The Sutton Registers of Baptisms, Marriages and Burials are missing from 1538, when registers were first kept, till August, 1636. After that date they have been well kept. The whole of the registers were transcribed by Mr. Bruce Bannerman and privately printed in 1915, and have been very well indexed. The first of the existing registers begins: " A register of Christenings, Marriages and Burialls, Ano 1636, beginninge the 10th day of June."

> Henry Wyche, being a non-Regent Maister of Arts in the University of Cambridge, was inducted by Thomas Pope into the Rectorie of Sutton, June 10th An. Dom. 1636, after a resignation made of the same Rectorie, by Jose Glover, who was much beloved of the most (if not of all) and his departure much lamented of the most, if not of All.

Henry Wyche died in 1678, and his widow appears to have carried off the register into Lincolnshire; but it was recovered by William Stephens, who became rector in 1690. The entry reads:

> May 7th 1703. Memorandum yt this Register of Sutton was carried away into Lincoln-shyre by Mrs. Wych, ye Widdow of Mr. Henery Wych, Rector of this p'sh [who

was buried Sept. 15th 1678 *crossed out*], and was restored to this p'ish by Mr William Wych, son to ye sd Henery, at ye int'mission of Mr William Stephens, now Rector of ye p'sh Church at Sutton.

But in ye meane time William Stewart, an honest man, who was Clark of this p'sh from Mr Wych's time til now, kept an account of ye Baptisms, Marriages, and Burialls, wh I am now goeing to transcribe over ye leafe.

Will. Stephens.

The register, therefore, appears to have been removed from Sutton by Mrs. Wych from 1678 till 1703, during which time there had been two other rectors of Sutton—George Roberts, 1678–1685, and Jeremiah Oakley, 1685–1690—besides William Stephens, who was instituted in 1690. It is a good thing that the clerk was an honest man and appears to have been business-like. The register shows that Henry Wyche, who became rector in 1636, was married in 1644 to " Ellen Quinell widdow of Robert quinnell of Asted." The baptisms of two sons and four daughters are registered, and also the marriage of one of the daughters, and finally the burial of Henry Wyche in 1678.

There are very few notes as to the trade or profession of the person registered, except between the years 1813 and 1837, when, in the case of baptisms, the trade or profession of the father is noted. There are, however, some interesting facts that can be gathered from-side notes in the register. For instance, in 1666 there were four deaths in a family called Thunderman, on June 6th, 26th, 28th, 28th, and a space is left between the two entries on the 28th, as if there had been more, but that they were never entered. Perhaps the deaths had occurred from plague, but the bodies had not been buried in the churchyard. The plague may have been lingering on in some places, though London had got over the worst of it.

Among the trades and professions of the fathers of those baptised between 1813 and 1837 there are bakers, bricklayers, butchers, carpenters, farmers, fishdealer, fisherman, fishmonger, gardeners, gentlemen, labourers, plasterers, plumbers, servants, shepherds, shoemakers, shopkeepers, tailors, and thatchers, while among those connected with horses, stage coaches and posting are postboys, toll men, wheelers, horsedealers, horsekeeper, horse patrol, footmen, collar-makers, corndealers, carters, and blacksmiths.

On September 5th, 1734, died " Linley, a black belonging to Mrs. Smith, by the name of Samuel."

On April 15th, 1677, was baptised John Sango, a Moor.

In 1784 a petition was presented protesting against soldiers, whose headquarters were at Croydon, being quartered in Sutton and Cheam, and saying that soldiers had been quartered on them for forty years (at one time from those who had headquarters at Epsom, but recently from those at Croydon), and asking that only those from Epsom should be sent to these places. There are a good many entries of soldiers as being buried, married, or being the fathers of children baptised between 1736 and 1800.

THE MANOR HOUSE stood on a site now bounded by the High Street, Benhill Avenue, Nursery Road and Manor Lane. The entrance was in Manor Lane, and the lodge stood a short way up the lane. There do not seem to be any pictures or descriptions of the building, but it seems to have been a large house and to have had a clock turret and a bell. There was a high brick wall to the grounds towards the High Street and part of Manor Lane. The house was pulled down about 1897. The last owner was Mr. George Orme. It is unfortunate that there are no records of a house so much associated with the history of Sutton.

In 1845, when the railway came to Sutton, Sutton Manor House was in the possession of Mr. Thomas Alcock, who developed a large part of the lands held by the Manor Estate, laying out roads and selling parcels of the land to builders and building societies, and doing a great deal for the development of the place. He was a generous benefactor to the church, giving liberally towards the rebuilding of the Parish Church, and towards the building and endowment of All Saints' Church at Benhilton. Mr. Alcock died in 1865.

SUTTON COURT, which stood in the Carshalton Road where the present Police Station now stands, was built by John Martindale, who had a stud of horses said to be the finest in Europe. It was a Georgian building, and was pulled down about 1899. A family of the name of Steel lived in it for many years.

THE LONDON INDUSTRIAL COLONY, the large building at the south end of the Brighton Road was originally built for the South Metropolitan Schools, for the pauper children of the Metropolitan Unions of Greenwich, St. Olaves, Camberwell and

Woolwich. The building was commenced in 1852, but took several years to complete, and hence got a local name of " linger and die." It had only just been completed—in fact part of it had only been inhabited for three weeks—when, at 2 a.m. on November 20th, 1856, a fire broke out in a blanket store and got a strong hold of the building before it was discovered. The children were all got out safely and without injury, but it was a cold night with a drizzling rain. Help was sent for, and in a short time some workmen arrived from Sutton and did what they could; but they could not do much owing to the shortage of water. In about an hour a fire engine arrived from Carshalton, and steps were taken to break away the roofs and so prevent the fire spreading to the rest of the building. After some hours' work this proved successful, and only the south wing (about one-third of the whole building) was destroyed. The building was covered by insurance, but not the furniture.

SUTTON LODGE (formerly known as Sutton Farm), is south of Sutton on the Brighton Road, nearly at Belmont, which was a very old farm with fine old barns and with a very picturesque Georgian house, with posts and rails in front, enclosing part of the old grass verge of the turnpike road. The farm was probably established on this spot for a very long time, but no records or account of it can be obtained.

Somewhere near Sutton Lodge was what was probably a small public-house, appearing on Roque's map as " Little Hell," which seems to show that it had not a very good reputation.

THE RECTORY is a modern building, but is on the site of the old one. The wall between the Rectory garden and the lane is old and constructed of squared chalk blocks, but has been much repaired with brickwork.

THE MARSHALL CHARITY, a very wealthy charity, owns a good deal of land in Sutton. John Marshall lived in Southwark and belonged to the Bakers' Company. The family originally came up from Lincolnshire and settled in Southwark. John Marshall made his will in 1627 and died in 1631. He left a good deal of property in land, and the income from this land was to accumulate until it reached the sum of £700, when a church was to be erected in Southwark to be called Christ Church. It was an unsettled time then, and it was twenty years before the church was commenced. Owing to settlements, resulting from a bad foundation, the church has had to be rebuilt since then, but it still stands as Christ Church, Southwark. The land he left consisted of some land in Lincolnshire; land in Southwark, on which the Borough High Street now stands; $3\frac{1}{2}$ acres in Newington; and this land in Sutton. The Sutton land is in two portions. One part is the area bounded by High Street, Oakhill Road, both sides of Brunswick Road, both sides of Marshall's Road, and two blocks in Benhill Street. The other part on the south side of the railway is the portion of the Brighton Road from Cedar Road to Cavendish Road, and part of Cavendish Road. It is now a very wealthy charity, and expends its income in building new churches, repairing and adding to old churches, and augmenting very small stipends of clergy. The only requirement the recipients of these charities must have is that the living must be in the gift of the Bishop of the Diocese in question.

It is not known how John Marshall became possessed of this land in Sutton, as his family came from Lincolnshire, and all attempts to find his connection with Sutton have proved fruitless. The author has spent a good deal of time in the quest. The first baptism in the Cheam register of 1538 is of the son of a Bartholomew Marshall, and his family and descendants figure in the Cheam registers for a hundred years and then die out. Unfortunately the registers of Sutton for these dates have been lost, and no Marshall figures in the later ones. It seems most probable that he inherited the property or got it from his wife, but no connection can be found to the names of either any of his fore-fathers or his wife's family.

In coaching days Sutton was a very busy place, with carriages, post chaises and stage coaches passing through it on their way to Sussex and to Brighton. It is recorded that twenty stage coaches passed through it in a day. Of course, too, as the church registers show, this gave a great deal of employment to ostlers and all others that had to do with horses.

THE INNS, too, were very busy at that time with coaches and carriages coming and going. The " Cock " must have been established before the Brighton Road was made a toll-road in 1755, as there is the register of the baptism of a daughter of Francis and Mary Wilson " at the Cock alehouse " in 1733; but it is not known if the " Cock " then stood on its present site or not, though it probably did. The present building is well beyond the edge of the Thanet Sands, so must have had a deep well to obtain water. The "Cock" must have been a busy place, especially on racing days, as it was a good "pull-up" on the way to the races, and it figures several times in old prints. The name of the inn may also indicate that cock-fighting took place in the neighbourhood. A sign-post stretched across the street, and the toll-gate originally stood just beside the inn, and was removed to a new position further south, between Egmont Road and Sutton Lodge, where it stood till it was finally abolished in 1882. The old inn was pulled down and rebuilt about thirty-five years ago.

The "Red Lion" is another old inn that was mentioned in the register, but this time it records a tragedy: "1799, July 25th. John Chart, 50, dropt down dead at the Red Lion. Registered 28th August, 1800."

Another inn is the "Greyhound," which stood in the High Street, and like the "Cock" had a sign across the street, which still remains. The building itself was rebuilt a few years ago.

The "Cricketers" stands in the Sutton High Street, and was a very picturesque wooden house. Probably it was an old half-timber building and the covering of boarding was put on about 1790, the date when so much of this boarding was used to prevent wet getting in between the timber framing and the "rye-dough" filling.

Another inn that was covered with weather-boarding was the "Plough," on the Sutton Common Road.

We hear a great deal about the present dangers of the roads, but they were not quite safe before the coming of the motor-car, for among the burials of 1800 is "December 25th, James Turner (killed by a cart wheel passing over his body at Mitcham)."

THE NEW TOWN.

The district round Lind Road, originally called Jenny Lind Road after the great singer Jenny Lind, who was at the height of her popularity in 1847-48, was laid out about that time. It was just on the Thanet Sands, so water would be obtainable. The chief development of Sutton seems to have been in this district from 1845, when the railway came, till 1863, when the Sutton Water Co. was incorporated and made building possible on the chalk and other districts away from the water-bearing area.

THE SUTTON WATER CO. began to supply water on January 1st, 1864, and must have started as quite a small district, as the revenue received for the water supplied during the first quarter of 1864 only amounted to £11 14s. 2d., though the first report, issued in December, 1863, states that "pipes are laid down for supplying nearly the whole of the principal inhabitants in Sutton and Cheam with water."

During 1867 pipes were laid and water supplied to a considerable portion of the Parish of Carshalton.

During 1868 7,582 yards of main were laid in Morden, Carshalton and Sutton. Between 1861 and 1871 Sutton more than doubled its population.

During 1878 the mains were extended through the village of Banstead.

During 1896 and 1897 new mains were put along Gander Green Lane and the London-Epsom Road for better supply to Morden, Ewell and North Cheam districts.

THE SUTTON GAS CO. was formed in 1857, and was amalgamated with the Wandsworth and District Gas Company in 1931.

THE SUTTON ELECTRICITY CO. was formed in 1899, as the County of Surrey Electrical Power Distribution Co. Ltd., and in 1904 the name was changed to the South Metropolitan Electric Tramway and Lighting Co. Ltd. The supply has been taken over by the London and Home Counties Joint Electricity Authority.

The lighting supply actually commenced in 1902.

From July, 1932, to March, 1936, the number of consumers has more than doubled, and during the same period the apparatus installed in the premises has been nearly quadrupled.

SOUTH SUTTON.

The first of the new houses to be built on the south side of the railway was Wellesley Lodge, which was built in 1861 by Mr. Montgomery Martin. In 1808 Mr. Martin's father was a secretary to Sir Arthur Wellesley, who at that time was Chief Secretary for Ireland. Mr. Montgomery Martin held appointments in India, Australia, Hong Kong and the West Indies, and wrote a book on *The British Colonies*, in fourteen volumes of Imperial quarto. While at Wellesley Lodge he wrote *The*

Wellington Supplementary Dispatches, twelve volumes of which have been published. 250,000 copies of his various works are said to have been issued.

It is interesting to note from the old directories how the roads gradually developed after it was possible to obtain water. Before the water mains were laid down in 1863 there were no houses south of the " Cock " except the tollgate and Sutton Lodge. By 1869 in the Brighton Road there were eight houses between the railway and the toll-gate on the east side, and one house, Wellesley Lodge, on the west side. By 1878 this had increased to eighteen houses on the east side and thirty-seven on the west side. In Cheam Road, in 1869, there were four houses on the north side and two on the south, but by 1878 these had increased to thirteen on the north side and twelve on the south. In Carshalton Road, in 1869, there were eleven houses on the north side and six on the south, and in 1878 there were twelve on the north and eleven on the south. In Cedar Road, in 1869, there were six houses on the south side and none on the north. By 1878 this had become twelve on the south and two on the north. Cavendish Road did not exist in 1869, but had two empty houses in it in 1878. In Cheam Road, in 1878, Church Farm, Sutton, extended on the north side from the High Street to Robin Hood Lane. In Grove Road, in 1869, there were two houses on the north side and seven on the south; in 1878 fifteen on the north and fourteen on the south. Mulgrave Road, in 1869, had ten houses on the north and five on the south, and in 1878 twenty-seven on the north side and eight on the south.

THE WAR MEMORIAL in Sutton was erected in 1921 by public subscription, from designs by Mr. J. S. W. Burmester, F.R.I.B.A. A piece of ground was purchased by the War Memorial Committee as a site for the memorial, adjoining another piece of nearly three acres which had been bought in 1914. Another piece of ground was presented in 1921 by Sir Ralph Forster and Messrs. Chas. Wright and Chas. Wall, which was part of the ground of a house called Manor Lodge. A further piece of ground was presented by Mr. Chas. Wright in 1931, and the whole of the memorial ground was called " Manor Park "; but it must not be confused with the site of the original Sutton Manor, which stood further north than Manor Lane.

War Memorial, Sutton.

RECREATION GROUNDS and open spaces are well provided in Sutton and Cheam, as there are 216 acres of parks and pleasure grounds, and forty-six acres of allotments, and the Borough is bounded on the south by the open North Downs and on the west side is Nonsuch Park. The largest ones are the Rose Hill (Dollar Estate), sixty-four acres; Rose Hill (Rose Hill Estate), thirty-five acres; Cheam Recreation Ground and Bethell Park (presented by Mrs. Bethell of Cheam Park), fifty-five acres; Glebe Land, Sutton Common Road, sixteen acres; Sear's Recreation Ground, Cheam (bequeathed by Mr. Sear of " The Quarry," Cheam), $7\frac{1}{2}$ acres; Cuddington Recreation Ground, twenty-five acres; Benhill Recreation Ground, five acres; and numerous private athletic and cricket grounds and tennis courts.

" The Green " in Sutton was allotted to the parish in 1810.

THE HIGHFIELDS ESTATE, on the eastern edge of Sutton, south of the railway, is actually in the parish of Carshalton, but it is so much part of Sutton that it may be mentioned here. This estate was laid out for building in 1905. Up to that time Eaton Road was the most easterly road in that part of the town, and there was no outlet from it towards Carshalton on the east until Hillcroome Road was made to give access to the estate from Sutton. Up to that time the estate consisted of several large fields of lavender, which was grown to be distilled into perfume at Mitcham, and to become the well-known " Mitcham Lavender." They were very beautiful fields, and the sight and perfume of them on a summer evening, when they were in full flower and the shadows of the clouds passed over them, was a thing not easily to be forgotten.

THE SUTTON CRICKET CLUB was first started in 1861, and the ground was lent by Mr. H. L. Antrobus, but was bought by the Club in 1901. One of the pavilions is part of the original Sutton railway station.

LOCAL PAPERS. By 1870 Sutton had become large enough to have a newspaper of its own.

In July, 1869, the *Croydon Advertiser and East Surrey Reporter* contained news of Sutton, and about the middle of 1870 the *Sutton Advertiser* was first published as a separate Sutton paper.

This was followed by the *Sutton Herald*, which was first published in 1878.

The Sutton and Epsom Mail was first published in 1922, and is now continued as the *Sutton Times and Cheam Mail*.

The *Cheam Times* was first published in 1929, and has a local edition for Worcester Park, and another for Stoneleigh.

SUTTON HIGH STREET used to be very pretty, and the author remembers cycling home to London, where he lived, one lovely summer evening about 1890, and running easily downhill from Banstead, was impressed with the picturesqueness of the High Street. On the east side there were the garden walls of some houses with trees overhanging the footpath; some quaint houses; the signs of the " Cock " and the " Greyhound " across the road; and beyond lay the extensive view all over London. When, a few years afterwards, he was looking for some new place in which to live, his thoughts returned to that view, and in 1895 he came to live in Sutton. When the character of the High Street was changing, several attempts were made, by petitions, etc., to have some of the attractive features retained, one being to make a circus where the Cheam and Carshalton roads cross the High Street; but all attempts were in vain, the prospect of immediate gain over-riding everything, and unfortunately all the beauties of the High Street have gone.

LOCAL GOVERNMENT. Cheam Parish Council, under the Epsom Rural Council, was formed in 1894, and continued until Cheam and Sutton were amalgamated in 1928.

Sutton became a Local Government District in 1882 and an Urban District Council in 1894. Unfortunately, the early Urban Council had very little vision as to what the future of the town would be, and no thought was taken to preserve the beauties of the place; everything was given up to immediate gain. There is no doubt that preserving the beauties of a town actually pays well in the long run, although there may be a temporary loss. To give an example. The author's grandfather was on the Town Council of Edinburgh early in the last century, when Prince's Street and the New Town of Edinburgh were being laid out. The original scheme was to build on both sides of Prince's Street. The author's grandfather opposed this, and led a movement that only one side of Prince's Street should be built on, so that the beautiful view of the Castle should be preserved, although all the money that could be obtained by selling one side of the street for building sites would be lost. The movement was successful, in spite of great opposition, and Prince's Street became one of the most beautiful streets in the world, attracting thousands of tourists every year to the town, and bringing in more money than could have been obtained by selling the building sites.

It was also unfortunate that Sutton Urban Council started with oppressive building bye-laws, while Cheam was under the much more up-to-date bye-laws of the Epsom Rural Council. These bye-laws are all amended now, but the old ones ran for many years, so that one could see the spot where one passed from Sutton to Cheam, simply by looking at the character of the buildings.

Sutton's first great development, about 1863, was also an unfortunate time, as domestic architecture was then in a transitional state. At the beginning of the nineteenth century the idea of putting damp-courses in walls, to prevent the damp from the earth creeping up the walls, had not been thought of, and therefore good-class houses had basements under the ground floor to keep the ground floor dry from rising damp. When damp courses to walls were introduced about 1830 to 1840, basements were no longer required to keep houses dry, but the conservative fashion for them was so strong that houses were still built with basements, or semi-basements, right on until about 1870, although the walls were built with damp-courses and basements were no longer required to keep houses dry. The first great development of Sutton was in this transitional period, and many of the houses built in this building boom, before 1870, were built with basements, and, of course, all without bathrooms, as before that date bathrooms were a rare luxury. This, of course, gave the town a bad start, and one from which it took a long time to recover; but after that the class of building became quite up-to-date, and many fine roads were laid out, with many good houses on them, and as the trees planted in the gardens grew, what had been bare common ground up to 1863 has become covered with trees and attractive-looking roads.

Cheam made its start in developing from the state of a village much later than Sutton did, and therefore escaped the "basement" period.

In 1928 Cheam was amalgamated with Sutton, and in 1934 Sutton and Cheam became a Borough. This process of amalgamating small places with larger towns near them was happening all over the country. Whether it was a wise movement time only will show. There may be a saving in administration, but at the same time the old traditions and the special requirements of each neighbourhood are lost, and the individual feels he has very little to do with the self-government of the place.

One wonders whether the old Saxon way of local government by small units was not, after all, the best one—small units which were represented in larger ones, which again were represented in still larger ones. It certainly worked well for some 1,300 years, but now that the old traditions are being lost, and the small units are all being merged in larger ones, the inhabitants feel they have very little voice in the local government, and lose all interest in the matter. It is suggested that it might have been a wiser thing to have improved on the old Saxon idea of small units, and to have made each ward a small separate unit with advisory powers only, these wards to have appointed representatives on larger bodies representing the old Saxon parishes, and these again being represented on the administrative body. In this way the individual and differing requirements of each district would have found expression in the central body. However, the Borough is now formed, and the town, having got over all the mistakes made in its growing days, is now using vision and foresight, making good the mistakes of the past, and making excellent provision for the difficulties of the future.

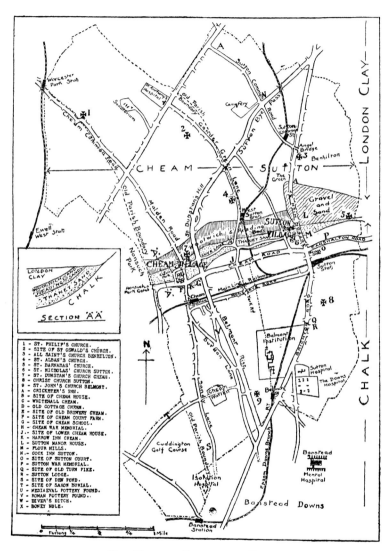

KEY PLAN OF SUTTON AND CHEAM.

ADDENDUM

Foreword

With the inclusion for the first time of this catalogue of events
witnessed in Cheam and Sutton from 1936 to the present day, I would
like to express my thanks to Mr. C.L. Quinton, for many years
Borough Librarian of Sutton and a long-standing resident,
Mr. I. Bradley, Reference Librarian in Sutton Central Library and the
late Mr. Robert P. Smith, for their valuable co-operation.

The aim in this record has been to give the maximum number of
events with the consequent minimum of essential wording about each.
It cannot claim to be exhaustive, owing to the difficulty of finding
and of combing all available sources.

It was thought desirable to give information in terse form and
arrange 'Cheam' and 'Sutton' in parallel columns, thus avoiding the
long-separated overlaps in the original work, items common to both
being spread over both columns.

Illustrations in books, etc., are mentioned under the relevant items.
A list of books and other works consulted is at the end.
A new index, revising that in the original book and including the
addition, is also at the end.
Sporting events are excluded, as are events relevant to Worcester Park.

Words following / indicate the source for the preceding information.

Dates	Cheam	Sutton
1936	Cheam Park acquired (For Cheam House see p.1.)	Gastro-enteritis epidemic
1936–37	Mayors of Borough of Sutton and Cheam: *see p.8; also Souvenir brochure*, p.33	
1937	Borough becomes, with that of Epsom and Ewell, owners of Nonsuch Park	
1938	Swimming baths, Malden Road, opened	
1939	Branch Library, Ridge Road, North Cheam, opened	B.B.C. TV 'At Home' programme featured Sutton
1940–41		War damage: to St. Nicholas, All Saints Benhilton, and Belmont Station

Dates	Cheam	Sutton
	Population estimate published	
1942	St. Andrew's Church, Northey Ave: Church House built/ *St. Andrew's Cheam* (booklet) 1968	
1944	*Greater London Plan,* by Patrick Abercrombie, published	
1945	Parliamentary Borough of Sutton and Cheam constituted	
1948		*Town guide to Sutton* published
1949		Baptist Church: glass in 'south' (actually west) window, by Miss D. Marion Grant/booklet (see 1969)
1951	Population estimate published Surrey Development Plan	
1952	Telephone Exchange and Post Office, Grove Road, Alan Dumble, architect	
1953	Borough Development Plan Coronation of Elizabeth II (Borough participated) Surrey Development Plan (see also 1962)	
1955	(Aug, 21) Anniversary (21st) celebrations of creation of Borough of Sutton and Cheam; Borough *Souvenir brochure;* (Sept. 8) Sutton and Cheam Advertiser, *Souvenir issue*	
		The Rev. R. W. Sharpley becomes Lord of the Manor of Sutton/R. P. Smith, p. 57
	St. Andrew's Church: Tweddle Hall built, main hall extended	Gas manufacture ceased
1957–58		Lilley & Skinner, 114 High Street; M. Egan, architect Willerby Tailoring, 116a High Street; C.J. Epril, architect
1959		Friends' Meeting House, rear of 7 Worcester Gardens, Brighton Road, opened; Mrs. Winifred Maddock, architect (see

Dates	Cheam	Sutton
		also '1970')
	Sutton and Cheam Society (for preservation of amenity) founded	
1959–61		Royal Marsden Hospital, Downs Road; Lanchester & Lodge, architects
1960		*History of Sutton,* by Robert P. Smith, first published
1960–64		Refugee Family Rectory, St. Nicholas, Beech Tree Place; E. F. Starling, architect Committee existed
1961	St. Andrew's Church: Scout Hall built	*History of Sutton,* 2nd ed.
1962	Public Library, Church Road, off Malden Road, opened; P. Masters and A. Pereira, architects	Civic Offices, 3 Throwley Road (illusn., *Official guide*); Owen Luder partnership, architects Helena House (office building), High Street (opposite The Green); Morgan & Branch, architects
	I. Nairn & N. Pevsner, *Surrey* (Bldgs. of England series), published; gives important buildings in all parishes	
	Sutton and Cheam Development Plan: Exhibition (Plan afterwards abandoned)	
1963	Population estimate published–78, 770, compared with that of 1935, 76, 772.	
	Wellesley Lodge opened as elderly people's home	
circa 1963		Methodist Church, Marshall's Road, renamed 'St. George's Church'
1964	St. Andrew's Church: Aitken Hall built	'Sutton' railway engine purchased (commemorating railway to Sutton 1845)
1964–65		Sutherland House (office building), 29 Brighton Road, Robert J. Wood & Partners, architects

Dates	Cheam	Sutton
1965	(April 1) London Borough of Sutton set up (including the former Borough of Sutton and Cheam and other boroughs) (Sutton and Cheam parliamentary constituency remains)	
	'Queen Victoria' public house, Church Hill Road, 'North Cheam'; E.S. Boyer & Partners, architects	Chaucer Gardens (housing development) (illusn. /Kennedy) Brambleacres (old house, 55 Worcester Road, and extension, Overton Road), elderly ladies' home, opened Harold Wilson Hall, Stayton Road
		Sentinel House (office building), 16–22 Sutton Court Road; Robert J. Wood & Partners, architects W.H. Smith & Son, High Street; Own Luder Partnership, architects
1965–68		domestic (mostly flat) buildings (about 17) (see Sutton Public Library's 'New buildings' list)
?1966 or before	Sutton District Council of Churches' *The Churches of Sutton and Cheam,* map leaflet, published	
1966	Willow Manor, Westfield Road (flats)	All Saints, Benhilton: centenary
		Gibson Mausoleum, St. Nicholas' churchyard, restored *History of Sutton* (above), 3rd ed. (current to date, 1970 Sept.)
1966–67		*List of buildings of architectural interest,* by H.V. Molesworth Roberts, typescript, photocopied.
1967	Pyl Brook flooding Whitehall (house)	Eagle Star House (office building), High Street,

Dates	Cheam	Sutton
	becomes Whitehall Galleries	opened: Owen Luder Partnership, architects Stanley Dean, Borough Librarian, died
1967–68/70	*Homefield Preparatory School: to Western Road; centenary*	
1968		Town Centre Redevelopment Plan approved Devonshire Primary School Greenshaw High School, Grennell Road; Sir John Burnet, Tait & Partners, architects
1968 (onward)	Greater London Development Plan 'Twinning' with Wilmersdorf, Germany	
1969		Baptist Church, Cheam Road; centenary of original foundation; *Past–present–future,* 1969 (*With* An architectural history, by H.V. Molesworth Roberts) Benhill Avenue housing estate begun Boots Chemists, High Street Health Centre, Robin Hood Lane Salvation Army: bldg. in Benhill Ave. (N. side, opposite Warwick Road) demolished; ex-Congregational Church (1859), same road (visible from High Street), recently factory, now theirs Synagogue (converted houses), 14 Cedar Road, opened
1970		J. R. Lamplugh becomes Lord of the Manor

Conservation Area
designated and approved/
Technical Office

Civic Centre published
Friends' Meeting House,
10 Cedar Road (to
replace earlier, see '1959')
opened
*Official guide and
directory* by London
Borough of Sutton

Prefabricated housing
schemes: U.S. delegations
visit

REFERENCE WORKS
(not specifically cited under relevant source
sign '/' as above).

General
1954–55   Borough of Sutton and Cheam *Year Book*
1955   Sutton and Cheam Advertiser, *A Souvenir* (issue) to mark
Sept. 8   the 21st anniversary &c.
1956   Kerslake, G., The Borough: ... a regional survey, typescript
     and illusns.
     I. Nairn and N. Pevsner, *Surrey*,
1969   Sutton Public Library, *New buildings in Sutton and
Cheam,* typescript, (1969)
1970   London Borough of Sutton, *Official guide and directory*
Sutton only
(after 1965)
     Kennedy, F.J., *Recent developments in Sutton* (in Inst. of
Mech. Engineers, conference paper)
1969   Baptist Church: *see* in main list, above
     Cheam
1968   St. Andrew's (Presbyterian) Church, Cheam, *St. Andrew's
Cheam,* booklet

Some buildings referred to in the original work
Based on plan in original work, p. 105, with information from Mr.
Quinton.

Still existing:—

Cheam	Sutton
'Old Cottage', Broadway	Cricketers' Inn, High St. (east side)
Whitehall (house), now	Sutton Lodge, Brighton Road
Whitehall Galleries	(east side)
White House, Part Road	
(according to Mr. Quinton)	

Demolished, with *approximate* new sites:—

Brewery	Cheam Hall	Cock Inn	London Life House
Cheam Court Farm	Cheam Court flats	Flour mills	(?) Gaumont Cinema now W.H. Smith's
Cheam House	Parkside, west end	Manor House	Manor Lane, N. side between
Cheam Park (house)	Cheam Park (open space, part of)		Lodge and Lenham Roads (Mr. R.P. Smith's plan)
Cheam School (called 'Manor House' on O.S. map 1933)	Tabor Court, Tabor Gardens	Sutton Court	Police Station (p. 95. of original work)
		Turnpike, Brighton Rd.	by Elmbridge Close
Harrow Inn	High Street/ Station Way, E. corner		
Lower Cheam House	(?) Cheam Road/ Gander Green Lane, W. corner		

Manor House:
*see Cheam
School, above*

The **Conservation Area** for 'Cheam Village' (happy phrase!) takes in Station Way (north of the railway), High Street (near half), Ewell Road (to the Park), the Broadway, Malden Road nearly to Lumley Road, Park Lane to the west of these and Park Road to the east of them. This area includes most of the weather-boarded cottages, except two pairs further north on the west side of Malden Road.

Mayors 1936–71

BOROUGH OF SUTTON AND CHEAM:—

1936/7	Sidney Horatio Marshall
1937/8	Grahame Robertson Clegg
1938/9	John James Goossens
1939/40	George Herbert Dennis
1940/1	John George Kipling
1941/2	William Howard Crosland
1942/3	John James Goossens

1943/4	Frederick Charles Lohden
1944/5	Joseph Scott Horne
1945/6	Henry John Trickett
1946/7	James Henry Nelson Curtis
1947/8	William Tuckett Venton
1949/50	William Douglas Milne
1950/1	Dorothy Webster
1951/2	Frank Warren
1952/4	Kingsley Williams
1954/5	Daniel Patrick Sullivan
1955/6	Daisy Sparks
1956/7	William Leshaw Hasted
1957/8	David Philip Thomas
1958/9	Robert William Jenkins
1959/60	Frederick William Thompson
1960/1	Irene A. Cook
1961/2	Percy Philip Oscar Mitchell
1962/3	Henry John Trickett
1963/5	David Philip Thomas

LONDON BOROUGH OF SUTTON:–

1965/6	Andrew William Letts
1966/7	Thomas Frederick Gadd
1967/8	Leslie John Hill
1968/9	Frederick Charles Finch
1969/70	Frederick George Moore
1970/1	John Leslie Bott
1971/2	Eric W. Harding

List kindly supplied by the Mayor's Secretary.

INDEX